Violence, the Sacred, and Things Hidden

Breakthroughs in Mimetic Theory

Edited by William A. Johnsen

Violence, the Sacred, and Things Hidden

A Discussion with René Girard at Esprit (1973)

René Girard

Translated by Andrew J. McKenna

With a foreword by Andreas Wilmes

Michigan State University Press

East Lansing

This series is supported by Imitatio, a project of the Thiel Foundation.

☉ The paper used in this publication meets the minimum requirements of ANSI/NISO Z39.48-1992 (R 1997) (Permanence of Paper).

Michigan State University Press
East Lansing, Michigan 48823-5245

Library of Congress Cataloging-in-Publication Data

Names: Girard, René, 1923-2015, author. | McKenna, Andrew J., translator.
  | Wilmes, Andreas.
Title: Violence, the sacred, and things hidden : discussion with René
  Girard at Esprit (1973) / René Girard ; translated by Andrew McKenna,
  with an introduction by Andreas Wilmes.
Other titles: Breakthroughs in mimetic theory
Description: East Lansing : Michigan State University Press, [2021] |
  Series: Breakthroughs in mimetic theory | Includes
  bibliographical references and index.
Identifiers: LCCN 2021001041 | ISBN 9781611864069 (paperback) | ISBN
  9781609176815 (pdf) | ISBN 9781628954487 (ePub) | ISBN 9781628964424
  (Mobi/prc)
Subjects: LCSH: Girard, René, 1923-2015--Interviews. | Girard, René,
  1923-2015. Violence et le sacré. | Esprit (Paris, France : 1932) |
  Violence--Philosophy. | Mimesis in literature. | Philosophy, Modern. |
  Sacrifice.
Classification: LCC B2430.G494 A5 2021 | DDC 201/.76332--dc23
LC record available at https://lccn.loc.gov/2021001041

Cover and book design by Erin Kirk
Cover art © Ali Mazraie Shadi

Visit Michigan State University Press at www.msupress.org

Contents

Foreword

Andreas Wilmes

In November 1973, the French literary magazine *Esprit* publishes a special issue on René Girard's latest book, *Violence and the Sacred*. It features an introductory article by Alfred Simon, "Les Masques de la Violence" ["The Masks of Violence"], which, as noticed by Benoît Chantre, "fails to convey an impressive understanding of Girard's" anthropology.[1] Simon contends that although Girard's book impresses by its ability to capture the mechanisms of violence with a remarkably clear and unadorned style, it nonetheless fails to capture the "essence" of violence. "In a certain way, aiming to speak about violence amounts to aiming to speak the unspeakable."[2] Unlike Bataille, Artaud, or Blanchot, Girard does not seem to understand that one must sacrifice the clarity of writing style and struggle with the very limits of language to grasp the essence of violence. Simon's critique points to a major obstacle—which, to some extent, is still current in France—to the reception and understanding of Girard's thought.

The concluding article of the special issue is authored by one of Girard's first students at the John Hopkins University, namely Eric Gans. In his paper, Gans expounds his interpretation of mimetic desire as "Triangular Aesthetics." He also shows that Girard placed the chapters on mimetic desire in the middle of his book because, from a logical point of view, his conception of desire is the cornerstone of his theory of the genesis of archaic religion. To Girard, what distinguishes Man from other animals is his lack of an inborn violence inhibition mechanism. As stated by Gans: "To understand the violence that is in us, we must be able to describe, in terms of human experience, which is at once subjective and objective, the *loss* of animal non-violence under the pressure of some positive force,"[3] that is, we must describe the collapse of violence inhibition mechanisms in terms of mimetic desire. Hence, in contrast to Simon, Gans holds that Girard's theory of desire captures something important about the essence of human violence.

However, the highlight of the special issue is undoubtedly the "Discussion with René Girard," published for the first time in English in the present volume. Parts of the discussion are the transcript of a meeting that took place at the editorial offices of *Esprit* on June 26, 1973,[4] and that involved, along with Girard, François Aubral, Michel Deguy, Jean-Marie Domenach, Eugénie Luccioni, Maurice Mourier, Pierre Pachet, Michel Panoff, and Paul Thibaud. Little is known about what went on behind the scenes of the meeting. At any rate, it is worth noting that some of Girard's interlocutors, like Pachet and Aubral, already have written reviews of *Violence and the Sacred*.[5] Deguy and Domenach will have an ongoing interest for Girard's works and will play a significant role in the French reception of mimetic theory. At the beginning of the 1970s, Aubral, Deguy, and Thibaud are philosophers by training. Panoff, a former student of Claude Lévi-Strauss, is doing research in ethnology. Luccioni, who frequently collaborates with the magazine *Esprit*, is a psychoanalyst who worked with Jacques Lacan. Mourier and Pachet have a solid background in literature and are at the beginning of their careers as essayists and novelists. Domenach, at that time the director of *Esprit*, is a Catholic intellectual who has a strong interest in Greek tragedy (his book *Le Retour du Tragique* was published in 1967). One may easily surmise that the large number of participants to the 1973 meeting has been warranted by the many topics covered in *Violence and the Sacred*. With his third book, Girard goes beyond the domain of literary theory and does not hesitate to cross the traditional boundaries between various fields of academic research. Obviously, his interlocutors are puzzled by his multidisciplinary approach, of which they strive to assess the relevance and validity.

Concerning the discussion published by *Esprit*, one thing is for sure: Girard's text entitled "The Astounding Effectiveness of Christianity" ["La Formidable Efficacité du Christianisme"] was not the one he presented during the meeting. Prior to publication, Girard replaced the initial content of his presentation "with a text *in extenso* he had originally planned as a conclusion to *Violence and the Sacred*, but then strategically withdrew."[6] "The Astounding Effectiveness of Christianity" refers to nothing else than the biblical unveiling of the victimage mechanism, which gradually starts with the Old

Testament and reaches its zenith with the Gospel. It is the first text in which Girard expounds on his theories of Christianity which he will further develop and refine till the end of his career. That is why the 1973 discussion published in *Esprit* constitutes a genuine and most significant breakthrough in mimetic theory.

Readers already familiar with Girard's writings may easily spot the many commonalities between "The Astounding Effectiveness of Christianity" and book two of *Things Hidden Since the Foundation of the World* (1978). In fact, Oughourlian notices that the considerations on the Judeo-Christian writings in *Things Hidden* were already "sketched out in a discussion published in *Esprit* in November 1973."[7] What is more, a close comparative reading shows that Girard reused without the slightest amendments several passages from the 1973 discussion for his conversations with Lefort and Oughourlian (see "Appendix: Table of Passages"). To be sure, the examination of the Holy Bible carried out in 1978 is much more minute than "The Astounding Effectiveness of Christianity." Still, in outline, from the Old Testament to the Apocalypse, Girard's analyses in the two texts are remarkably similar.

As noted by Lefort and Oughourlian, a rather superficial reading of the *Esprit* discussion led some of Girard's contemporaries to believe that he aimed at defending the Holy Scriptures from a strictly humanistic and atheistic perspective.[8] However mistaken that reading is, it is nonetheless true that in 1973 Girard insists less on the miraculous features of the Christian Revelation than he will do in the late 1970s. Unlike the surrogate victim in archaic religion, Christ is not a victim turned into a god through the hallucinations of the violent mob. His death, as Girard puts it, is "the same thing [as] our death, a death that is completely separated from resurrection and with no relation to it. Christ does not play with life and death in the manner of the phoenix, of the Aztec gods, or Dionysus." What makes Christ extraordinary is His ordinary death on the cross. If that were not the case, the Passion of Jesus would merely be another instance of "the eternal game of sacralization." In essence, archaic myths are stories of persecution told from the point of view of the persecutors. Myths are texts that are unaware of their proper structure. They are texts shaped through the delusional state of the crowd, the cathartic effects of collective violence, and, ultimately, the ignorance of the innocence of the surrogate victim. To decipher myths, one has to part with the perspective they introduce. It is the blind spot of the texts that points to the rules of their interpretation. By revealing the founding murder, the Holy Scriptures break "away from the rules of ordinary textuality," that is, they display their "own exegetical functioning." In myths, the rules of interpretation are to be found outside of the text. In the Bible, the rules of interpretation are immanent to the text. Or, put differently, the text shows itself to be aware of its very own structure. Girard never argues that Christ's death on the cross and the extraordinary textuality of the Scriptures must be thought of as independent of any reference to transcendence. In effect, he states that "We have to see in Christ the *mysterious subject* of this text who compels violence to inscribe itself in his person, forces it to come out in the open, to objectify itself so as to become gradually inoperative." But it is only a few years later in *Things Hidden* that Girard will come to more straightforwardly explain why the mystery of Christ cannot be separated from the very logic of his reading of the Gospels. In a world still governed by archaic religion, the victimage mechanism works blindly. Men's ignorance (i.e., "*méconnais-sance*") ensures the self-regulating mechanisms of violence that are at the origin of their culture. Given that the closure of representation instituted through violence and the archaic sacred cannot be bypassed by ordinary human knowledge, the Christian Revelation of the victimage mechanism must be divine. As noted by Girard in 1978: "The authentic knowledge about violence and all its works to be found in the Gospels cannot be the result of human action alone."[9] Through His death on the cross and His resurrection on the third day, Jesus shows that the archaic sacred was nothing else than sacralized violence, and that a radically different kind of sacredness, a nonsacrificial sacredness based on love and the renunciation of violence, had arisen. What is more, it is only thanks to the miracle of resurrection that Jesus's disciples come to be capable of breaking away from the closure of representation of the victimage mechanism.

In any event, Girard already and fully endorses the transcendent nature of the Christian Revelation in 1973. "The gods of violence," he contends, "are demonetized by the announcement of a god of love." In contrast to Alfred Simon, he does not equate the essence of violence with the unspeakable. Rather, it is the transcendence of love that forces violence to reveal its true nature. Talking and thinking about violence today is not a matter of playing with the limits of language. It is not a matter of showing, like Bataille and Blanchot did, that the writings of the Marquis de Sade aim to go beyond the boundaries of human reason and strive to speak the unspeakable. To the contrary, it is in the Gospels, which are inspired by the transcendence of love, that language points to what goes beyond its own limits. On the one hand, the Christian Revelation of violence is clear and not deceitful. And yet, on the other hand, the very source of that Revelation goes beyond human comprehension. It is because he radically parts from the way his contemporaries think of violence with respect to the limits of language that Girard firmly dismisses "the old scandals reheated many times over" and "the old romantic follies boringly recycled" at his time. There is a real intellectual revolution here that, although better understood today than in the early 1970s, has probably not yet been fully appreciated and discussed.

On a different note, we may wonder why "The Astounding Effectiveness of Christianity" has been published in 1973 rather than as a conclusion to *Violence and the Sacred*. Also, we may wonder how the conclusion Girard initially planned but eventually withdrew relates to his third book. According to Chantre, Girard did not publish his first investigations on the Holy Scriptures in 1972 to foster properly scientific debates with anthropologists and ethnologists. With an explicitly religious conclusion, *Violence and the Sacred* might have been received very differently by Girard's peers. It is even highly likely that, to many readers, such a conclusion would have overshadowed the rest of the book. Especially under the French intellectual tyranny of the "*d'où parles-tu?*" many would have assumed that *Violence and the Sacred* boils down to a defense of Christianity disguised as science. Those explanations concur with the ones given by Girard in the following passage (omitted in the English translation) of *Things Hidden*:

> If I did not speak about the Christian text in *Violence and the Sacred*, it is because it would have been sufficient to evoke it to persuade most readers that I was indulging in a particularly hypocritical work of apologetics. No matter what happens, this is what people will not fail to say. It is nowadays agreed that all thought is

subordinated to more or less unavowable ideological or religious goals. And the most unavowable of all, of course, is to take an interest in the text of the Gospels, and to notice the formidable hold it exerts on our universe.[10]

At the time of its publication, "*Violence and the Sacred*, despite Girard's later claims, did not go unnoticed in France."[11] However, to his greatest disappointment, his envisioned discussion with anthropologists and ethnologists failed to happen. It is out of impatience and resignation, Chantre implies, that Girard eventually decides to publish his text on the Judeo-Christian writings in 1973.[12] On the one hand, thanks to the discussion published in *Esprit*, Girard's theories will reach a new audience, including, especially, Raymund Schwager.[13] On the other hand, just as Girard feared and expected, the sudden announcement of his Christian apologetics will elicit dismissive attitudes from anthropologists and ethnologists.

Notwithstanding its deferred publication, shall "The Astounding Effectiveness of Christianity" be regarded as the genuine conclusion of *Violence and the Sacred*? In 1974, Pierre

Manent answers in the affirmative.[14] Girard would have hidden the true conclusion of his book from his readers. By the same token, he would have concealed the transcendent source of a theory scientific in name only. Hence, the 1973 discussion would bring substantial discredit to what Girard claimed to have completed in *Violence and the Sacred*. In 1978, however, Girard explains that it was for the sake of honesty to his readers that he removed the planned conclusion on the Judeo-Christian writings:

> The thesis of the scapegoat owes nothing to any form of impressionistic or literary borrowing. I believe it to be fully demonstrated on the basis of the anthropological texts. That is why I have chosen not to listen to those who criticize my scientific claims and have determined to try to reinforce and sharpen the systematic character of my work, and to confirm the power of the scheme to reveal the genesis and structure of cultural phenomena.
>
> In effect, all that I did in *Violence and the Sacred* was to retrace, with all its hesitations, my own intellectual journey, which eventually brought me to the Judaeo-Christian [sic] writings, though long after I had become

convinced of the importance of the victimage mechanism. In the course of this journey, I remained for a long period as hostile to the Judaeo-Christian texts as modern orthodoxy could wish. But I came to the conclusion that the best way of convincing my readers was not to cheat on my own experience and to reproduce its successive stages in two separate works, one of which would deal with the universe of sacred violence, and the other with the Judeo-Christian aspect.[15]

Girard's explanation is also warranted in that readers must go through three stages to understand his "system": the theory of mimetic desire, then the hypothesis of the victimage mechanism, and finally the analysis of the Bible. It is not possible to go through these steps in a different order. As noted by Gans, to understand the proper logic of the victimage mechanism, a prior knowledge of mimetic desire is required. And, as stressed by Oughourlian, "To understand that the Gospels really do reveal all this violence, we have to understand first of all that this violence engenders the mythic meanings."[16] Girard expounds the three stages of his mimetic theory for the very first time in 1973. But he does not delineate them in a didactic way, which probably explains why the discussion published in *Esprit* led to some misunderstandings. Nonetheless, throughout the 1970s, Girard distinguishes the scientific presentation of his hypothesis of the victimage mechanism from his analysis of the Scriptures. The first sentences of the conclusion to *Violence and the Sacred* read:

> *Our inquiry on myths and rituals has come to an end.* This inquiry enabled us to formulate a *hypothesis that we now regard as warranted* and lies at the base of a theory of primitive religion. The extension of this theory towards Judeo-Christianity and culture in its entirety is already in progress. It will be left to a future study.[17]

In *Things Hidden*, book one is devoted to the "Fundamental Anthropology" while book two is devoted to "The Judeo-Christian Scriptures." And, as a matter of fact, book one is dealing "with the hypothesis of the scapegoat as an exclusively scientific one [*proprement et seulement scientifique*]."[18] Over the 1970s, Girard remained consistent regarding the distinction between the scientific and the religious part of his work. This aspect further supports the view that "The

Astounding Effectiveness of Christianity" shall not be read like the authentic but strategically concealed conclusion of *Violence and the Sacred*.

To Girard, the scientific and Christian dimensions of his work are interrelated yet distinct. In outline, following the rules of science amounts to using reliable concepts, introducing clear-cut hypotheses and a criterion to measure their validity—as shown by Girard throughout the 1973 discussion, it is explanatory power rather than Popper's demarcation criterion that applies to fundamental anthropology. Yet a discourse does not have to be fully aware of its own origins or conditions of possibility to be scientific. Girard's theory of archaic religion aims to show how to decipher the meaning of myths and rituals. However relevant, questions pertaining to the conditions of possibility of the method of decipherment at the core of the theory go beyond the question of what makes the theory scientific. Girard may thus contend that his theory must be evaluated according to scientific standards even though its historical conditions of possibility are to be found in Christian Revelation. By revealing the process of the sacralization of violence in archaic religion, Christianity desacralizes nature and paves the way to modern science. But even though science may forget about its origins, Girard never denies that science works by its own rules.

It is not quite certain that Girard made himself understood by his interlocutors in 1973. In the discussion, he vindicates in a provocative way the relation between science and Christianity ("Modern thought would then do well to think about those numerous desert excavators in Second Isaiah . . ."), which leads to reinforcing a significant and already existing disagreement with Aubral. In January 1973, Aubral published a very dismissive and sardonic book review of *Violence and the Sacred* in the journal *Les Cahiers du Chemin*. In his critique, he acknowledges the scientific ambitions of Girard's book, which, according to him, are nothing else than "chimeric."[19] Girard, he argues, is mainly cherry-picking examples that best fit the victimage mechanism hypothesis. To Aubral, *Violence and the Sacred* is a book devoid of methodology that completely disregards issues of scientific evidence as well as the most significant differences between literature, psychology, ethnology, and philosophy. The only concept developed "through four hundred fifty pages," he continues, is that of "founding violence," which boils down to an odd and irrelevant re-actualization of Hobbes's "war of all against all."[20] Not only does the anthropology of the English philosopher already contain the theory of mimetic desire ("And therefore if any two men desire the same thing, which nevertheless they cannot both enjoy, they become enemies . . ."), but he also was "less dogmatic" and naïve than Girard in that he did not conflate the state of nature with an actual founding event. Hobbes's reflections on violence were a necessary step towards political science—which, during the seventeenth century, had to free itself from theology—and social contract theory. In contrast, *Violence and the Sacred* would be a regression to theology, with the book's core idea of a founding murder being reminiscent of that of "original sin."[21] What is more, by leveling out cultural, historic, and social differences, Girard's conception of violence would turn out to be abstract and universalist. Ultimately, Aubral concludes, Girard is nothing but the "victim of the founding illusion of his failed system [*victime de l'illusion fondatrice de son système avorté*]."[22]

This surely explains why Girard's debate with Aubral at the editorial offices of *Esprit* was quite tense. However, more importantly, it is the discussion in full that gives Girard the opportunity to respond to the main objections raised by Aubral's book review. For instance, Girard argues that the social contract model, by dismissing the possibility that archaic religion may have a genuine social function (i.e., to put an end to the potentially endless cycle of vengeance), constitutes a major epistemological obstacle to anthropology. More generally, he takes the opportunity to stress that, far from being regressive, his endeavor in *Violence and the Sacred* was to solve problems specific to anthropological and ethnological research of his time. In the introductory presentation of his theory, he especially dwells on the issue of the unbridgeable gap between myths and rituals in Claude Lévi-Strauss. According to the latter, origin and creation myths "describe the shift from the continuous to the discontinuous"—that is, they describe the shift from an "indistinct whole" to a world where things are made discernable, categorizable, and comparable through human thought. The continuous refers to a set of data that is too compact and needs to be spaced out so that it can be grasped by the mind. Mythology, in other words, introduces "differential gaps."[23] It is on the side of differentiation. To Lévi-Strauss, ritual goes against the differentiating activity of human thought and thereby seeks "to undo what myth has accomplished."[24].Ritual, in other words, is entirely on the side of undifferentiation. From a structuralist perspective, mythology reveals "to us the conditions for the exercise of all thought," whereas ritual is not worthy of much interest.[25] Ultimately, the relationship between myth and ritual appears in a problematic and antinomic light. However, it is not Girard's aim to dismiss Lévi-Strauss's approach as a whole. As already mentioned in *Violence and the Sacred*, "Structuralism constitutes a negative but indispensable stage in the discovery of the sacred."[26] It is necessary to account for the structures highlighted by Lévi-Strauss on the basis of the undifferentiation (i.e., the continuous) he leaves at the margins of his writings. To that end, as Girard explains in 1973, it is pivotal to challenge the idea that mythology would mainly be on the side of differentiation, whereas ritual would be entirely on the side of undifferentiation. Actually, both myth and ritual pertain to the shift from undifferentiation to differentiation. In the former, we move from a state of original chaos to the differential gaps of culture. In the latter, the differential gaps of culture are transgressed for the ultimate purpose of being reaffirmed (in rites of passage, for instance, undifferentiation leads to re-differentiation). As Girard puts it at the beginning of the discussion:

> In myths as in rituals, it is the erasure of differences, by a mystery that is never explained, that allows them to appear or reappear more distinctly than ever, reinforced and stabilized. It is this passage through undifferentiation, culminating typically in the violence of sacrifice, that is the midwife to myriad subdivisions among groups, different seasons, etc.

In addition, it is important not to limit the relationship between the differentiated and the undifferentiated to a strictly logical and linguistic problem (i.e., the move from the continuous to the discontinuous). For, as we are reminded in the 1973 discussion, undifferentiation should not be thought of separately from violence (i.e., the violence of sacrifice, festivals, sexual transgressions, and so forth). Based on these observations, Girard is able to show that the hypothesis of the victimage mechanism goes beyond the aporias of structuralism by explaining the shift from undifferentiation to differentiation, that is to say, the shift from collective violence to the birth of the cultural and symbolic order. This point is quite important to him, as evidenced by the two articles on Lévi-Strauss he would publish a few years later.[27] Moreover, given that Girard's thoughts on undifferentiation and differentiation are paramount to demonstrate the novelty of his mimetic theory,[28] it is more than understandable that they are at the center of the 1973 discussion.

In the *Esprit* discussion, Girard vindicates the truth of the Gospels for the very first time. He also defends his scientific endeavor in *Violence and the Sacred* on the two fronts of the explanatory power of his theory and of his concept of violent undifferentiation as a means of complementing and overcoming Lévi-Strauss's structuralist approach. He further challenges Freudian and Lacanian theories, dwells on the historical context of tragedy, expounds his views on modern social struggles, sketches reflections on international relations and nuclear deterrence that not only prefigure *Things Hidden* but also his last book, *Battling to the End*. In sum, the discussion in *Esprit* is at the same time an intellectual tour de force by Girard, a text marking a new and decisive step in his intellectual journey, and a document concerning a very decisive phase in the French reception of his thought. It is time for English readers to discover this mind-blowing milestone in mimetic theory.

Notes

1. Benoît Chantre, "René Girard in France," *Contagion* 23 (2016): 26.

2. Alfred Simon, "Les Masques de la Violence," *Esprit* 11 (November 1973): 524.

3. Eric Gans, "Toward a Triangular Aesthetics," trans. Trevor Cribben Merrill, *Contagion* 24 (2017): 9. Article originally published in *Esprit*: Eric Gans, "Pour une Esthétique Triangulaire," *Esprit* 11 (November 1973): 564–581. In his introduction to the English translation of his article, Gans states: "Girard's explicit aim was to offer a model of how human culture as such—albeit viewed exclusively from the side of sacred ritual and neglecting the question of language—could have been born from the minimal trait of 'too much mimesis.'" See Eric Gans, "Introduction to 'Toward a Triangular Aesthetics,'" *Contagion* 24 (2017): 2.

4. Chantre, "René Girard in France," 57.

5. Pierre Pachet, "Pourquoi la violence?" *Quinzaine Littéraire* (July 16, 1972); and Pierre Pachet, "Violence dans la bibliothèque," Critique 28 (1972): 716–728. François Aubral, "René Girard: *La violence et le sacré*," *Les Cahiers du Chemin* 17 (January 15, 1973): 192–205.

6. Chantre, "René Girard in France," 28.

7. René Girard, *Things Hidden Since the Foundation of the World*, trans. Stephen Bann and Michael Metteer New York: Bloomsbury, 2016), 264.

8. Speaking to Girard, Oughourlian notices: "Your reading has been judged to be humanist because you attached great importance to 'Eli, Eli, lama sabactani' when you entered into a debate published in *Esprit* in 1973." Ibid., 223.

9. Ibid., 210.

10. René Girard, *Des choses cachées depuis la fondation du monde* (Paris: LGF, 1983), 246. My translation.

11. Chantre, "René Girard in France," 30.

12. "It is as if the silence with which the anthropologists and ethnologists greeted his theory made him understand that he would never really be discussed by them." Ibid., 28.

13. In his very first letter addressed to Girard (March 18, 1974), Schwager states: "I discovered your book *La violence et le sacré*, from

reading the journal *Esprit*." See René Girard and Raymund Schwager, *Correspondence 1974–1991*, trans. Chris Fleming and Sheelah Treflé Hidden (New York: Bloomsbury, 2016), 15.

14. Pierre Manent, "René Girard, la violence et le sacré," *Contrepoint* 14 (June 1974): 157–170.

15. Girard, *Things Hidden*, 169–170.

16. Ibid., 169.

17. René Girard, *La Violence et le Sacré* (Paris: Hachette Littérature, 1998), 463. My translation and my emphasis. Regarding this passage, there is a significant difference between the original French edition and the English translation. See René Girard, *Violence and the Sacred*, trans. Patrick Gregory (Baltimore: Johns Hopkins University Press, 1977), 309.

18. Girard, *Things Hidden*, 135.

19. François Aubral, "René Girard: *La violence et le sacré*," 203.

20. Ibid., 203–204.

21. Ibid., 204.

22. Ibid., 205.

23. Lucien Scubla, "Lévi-Strauss and Girard on Mythology and Ritual," in *The Palgrave Handbook of Mimetic Theory and Religion*, ed. James Allison and Wolfgang Palaver (New York: Palgrave Macmillan, 2017), 88. To Lévi-Strauss, "discontinuity is achieved by the radical elimination of certain fractions of the continuum." See Claude

Lévi-Strauss, *The Raw and the Cooked*, trans. John and Doreen Weightman (New York: Harper & Row Publishers, 1969), 52. According to Girard, this "radical elimination" must be explained by the victimage mechanism.

24. Scubla, "Lévi-Strauss and Girard," 88.

25. Ibid., 88. Regarding this difference between myth and ritual, see Claude Lévi-Strauss, *The Naked Man*, trans. John and Doreen Weightman (Chicago: University of Chicago Press, 1990), 625–695.

26. Girard, *Violence and the Sacred*, 242.

27. René Girard, "Differentiation and Reciprocity in Lévi-Strauss and Contemporary Theory" and "Violence and Representation in the Mythical Text," in *To Double Business Bound* (Baltimore: John Hopkins University Press, 1978), 155–198.

28. For a philosophical perspective on this topic, see Andreas Wilmes, "Portrait of René Girard as a Post-Hegelian," *Philosophical Journal of Conflict and Violence* 1, no. 1 (2017): 57–85.

References

Aubral, François. "René Girard: *La violence et le sacré*." *Les Cahiers du Chemin* 17 (January 15, 1973): 192–205.

Chantre, Benoît. "René Girard in France." *Contagion* 23 (2016): 13–61.

Gans, Eric. "Introduction to 'Toward a Triangular Aesthetics.'" *Contagion* 24 (2017): 1–3.

———. "Pour une Esthétique Triangulaire." *Esprit* 11 (November 1973): 564–581.

———. "Toward a Triangular Aesthetics." Translated by Trevor Cribben Merrill. *Contagion* 24 (2017): 5–21.

Girard, René. *Things Hidden Since the Foundation of the World* [1978]. Translated by Stephen Bann and Michael Metteer. New York: Bloomsbury, 2016.

———. *To Double Business Bound*. Baltimore: John Hopkins University Press, 1978.

———. *Violence and the Sacred* [1972]. Translated by Patrick Gregory. Baltimore: Johns Hopkins University Press, 1977.

Girard, René, and Raymund Schwager. *Correspondence 1974–1991*. Translated by Chris Fleming and Sheelah Treflé Hidden. New York: Bloomsbury, 2016.

Lévi-Strauss, Claude. *The Naked Man*. Translated by John and Doreen Weightman. Chicago: University of Chicago Press, 1990.

———. *The Raw and the Cooked* [1964]. Translated by John and Doreen Weightman. New York: Harper & Row Publishers, 1969.

Manent, Pierre. "René Girard, la violence et le sacré." *Contrepoint* 14 (June 1974): 157–170.

Pachet, Pierre. "Pourquoi la violence?" *Quinzaine Littéraire* (July 16, 1972).

———. "Violence dans la bibliothèque." *Critique* 28 (1972): 716–728.

Scubla, Lucien. "Lévi-Strauss and Girard on Mythology and Ritual." In *The Palgrave Handbook of Mimetic Theory and Religion*, edited by James Allison and Wolfgang Palaver, 85–93. New York: Palgrave Macmillan, 2017.

Simon, Alfred. "Les Masques de la Violence." *Esprit* 11 (November 1973): 515–527.

Wilmes, Andreas. "Portrait of René Girard as a Post-Hegelian." *Philosophical Journal of Conflict and Violence* 1, no. 1 (2017): 57–85. doi:10.22618/TP.PJCV.20171.1.95007.

Translator's Introduction

Andrew J. McKenna

Near the very end of *Violence and the Sacred*, René Girard
summarizes his scientific claims for "a rigorous definition of
such terms as *divinity*, *ritual*, *rite*, and *religion*. Any phenomenon associated with acts of remembering, commemorating,
and perpetuating a unanimity that springs from the murder of a surrogate victim can be termed 'religious'" (315).
Throughout the discussion he refers to all this as "le reli-
gieux," concerning myths and rituals, especially sacrificial
ones, overt or covert, in his exploration of ancient and archaic religions. I have translated this substantivized adjective,
a more common practice in French, as "religious thought,"
perhaps misleadingly because throughout the discussion his
aim is to bring to the light of critical analysis what is not
thought through in the beliefs and practices of the cultures

hosting them, nor by most studies devoted to them. The singular exception is biblical revelation, Jewish and Christian, that inaugurates a focus on the victims of sacrificial rites and that he argues is what makes his analyses available. Girard himself has duly recognized his claims as "enormous" and as such they are predictably as attractive to some as they are repulsive to others, as they aim at a unified theory of cultural origins and mystified organization that is filled out in *Things Hidden Since the Foundation of the World* and subsequent writings. The result has been labeled by some among both advocates and adversaries as a Grand Unifying Theory, a Theory of Everything, an audacious project to which academic departments in our disciplinary fortresses are understandably averse. I will not review these matters, as Andreas Wilmes has expertly appraised them in his own introduction.

Instead I choose to engage with François Aubral's highly critical review of *Violence and the Sacred*, as referred to in a footnote in the discussion, which Andreas Wilmes kindly forwarded to me, and which enables me to focus on certain still-relevant issues raised by Girard's work. In this I am following Girard's example in his opening remarks, where he expresses gratitude for objections to his work as occasions for further clarifications. For Aubral's account of *Violence and the Sacred* is overall astute, accurate, and still pertinent; it consists of reliable paraphrase of its contents that are scrupulously bolstered by recourse to relevant quotes; it's as good as I've seen anywhere. His principle objection is to the sweep of Girard's claims, as he ranges through anthropology, psychoanalysis, and literature to make his case against "religion," and this is indeed a "slippery" term, as James Alison notes in his contribution to the study of Neolithic sites (197).

Religion is indeed a dangerous term, as we find today that its role in culture is disputed, and sometimes violently, all over the globe. I shall not argue here the case Girard makes for his hypothesis and for its scientific ambitions; that is for the reader to judge, and hopefully in the light of his subsequent work and the vast archive of research it has stimulated. I shall address Aubral on the matter of literary studies, my own field of teaching and research, but precisely as they necessarily bleed into data and issues that are presumed to be the preserve of other academic disciplines.

For literature departments are interdisciplinary by default, and hopelessly so, for their subject matter, in novels and plays, for instance, as they concern human interaction, involves psychology, sociology, history, philosophy (at least as ethics), and religion as well. By definition, or rather by lack thereof, literary studies are in a state of acute, chronic boundary collapse. When Girard was teaching at Johns Hopkins, leading contenders for eminence Northrop Frye and Kenneth Burke were already making forays into anthropology and scriptural studies. And Girard came to literary criticism somewhat by accident. His academic degree from Indiana University is in history, which followed upon his graduate studies at the Ecole des Chartres, whereby he was trained as paleographer, a student of ancient and medieval texts. In his early employment, he found himself to be one of those prize possessions of language departments, "a native speaker," so he was asked to teach French literature.

As he ranged over the French literary canon, he reports that, where literary humanism tended to focus on the individual genius of this or that writer, he detected a pattern, a structure, which was common to the novels and plays assigned to his purview. When not wrestling with esthetic issues, comparative literature studies at the time were mostly doing literary history, largely devoted to tracing influences; Girard found the novels were studying him, unpacking, as it were, his psyche. In his first book, *Deceit, Desire, and the Novel*, he accomplished what amounts to a decoding of desire, as informed by literary masterpieces, which portrayed desire not as a relation of subjects to objects but as issuing from the agency, real or imagined, conscious or not, of models, mediators; desire is mimetic, in sum, a fact that, upon reflection, few people would dispute. Our greatest novels in the tradition of realist narrative, beginning with *Don Quixote*, were engaged in revealing the romantic delusion of an individual self as the origin of its motivations and actions. This book was already exceptional for its conspicuous and ardent truth claims about literature, though not without implications for anthropology broadly conceived, namely human self-understanding.

In *Violence and the Sacred*, he similarly decodes violence, deciphering the violence that is encrypted in myth and ritual, in behaviors and institutions. We wrongly conceive violence in terms of punctual eruptions, as coming from the outside, as alien to our natively pacific disposition, whereas he finds it as a relation of mimetic rivalry leading to conflict, such as we find it in his analysis of *Oedipus Tyrannos* in *Violence and the Sacred* (68–88). Rationality is relationality for Girard, as indeed it is for Lévi-Strauss, with the defining difference that Girard bases it on our unacknowledged relation to the victim of violence. Girard's idea is that we find the best hermeneutic models in our literary canon, which we need to remember is heir to the biblical one, as a category of texts endowed over time with cultural authority.

Aubral is emphatic about such a claim: "René Girard, critique littéraire?" While acknowledging Girard's literary culture, he asserts that his "ethnological observations deny the specificity of what is literary ('le littéraire'), making the symbolism of writing ('écriture,' a fetish word for the French: 'writerliness'?) coincide with a possible field of truth. . . . In itself, literature is a given ('un donné') that different branches of scientific practices should approach as an object to circumscribe, interpret and understand. As such it is insufficient to support a theory as ambitious as Girard's" (200–201). Aubral's strictures about literary specificity can remind us of

Baudelaire's appraisal of Balzac, where he remarks that all the things the novelist's critic's hold up as his defects are in fact his merits. Aubral's conception of literary studies fits the standard academic model of literature as an object of scrutiny requiring tools of other disciplines to interpret it. Girard flips the script, endowing our literary masterpieces with interpretive agency and authority; he attaches a higher value to literary excellence than anyone before. As we read them, they read us, they tell us our story at best, when not emanating from romantic delusions. They are in advance of our social sciences, which are not to be discounted; but great writings are not dependent upon them for their explanation.

Whence Girard's properly anthropological sense of literature as human self-understanding, as a wellspring of truth about ourselves that we prefer to ignore, or outright deny. This is especially the case for Americans with our besetting myth of "individualism," which is in fact a neologism coined by de Tocqueville, an altogether "amateur" for social sciences yet to be born. Tocqueville came up with this term to explain what Democracy in America portended, somewhat ominously, for the future of free and equal self-governing. Freud's famous observation that "the ego is not master in his own house" comes to mind, not because of intrapsychic drives, but because of others, whose role in our lives are occluded. Girard's idea of our interdividuality, his only neologism, conforms more realistically to what we conceive as a self in a field of silos, as if we were in a forest where there are only trees, the ones beside the others and competing for resources. Mikkel Borch-Jacobsen has shown the mimetic forces at work in Freud's own writings, including the founding father's efforts to obfuscate them, as well as to exclude rival theories, including those of his own disciples. There is already here a "theater of envy," which is how Girard was later to define the plays of Shakespeare: The father disputes his heritage with his sons, who dispute it among themselves thereafter. Something Oedipal is going on in the history of psychoanalysis, but it's about rivalry of doubles—Laius/Oedipus, Oedipus/Tiresias, Oedipus/Creon; then Eteocles/Polyneices—fueling the model/obstacle impasse, not internal compulsions. Greek tragedy has more to tell us about human interaction than our individualistic psychologies have been able to imagine.

Elsewhere, Aubral reproaches Girard for comparing the

organization of a Bororo village to what we can imagine as a crowd whose attention is drawn by a street brawl. "Thus, Girardian violence enters among the Bororo" (202). But Girard's point is that the Bororo village circle is arranged and enforced in a hierarchical order, where everyone's place is fixed, such that there cannot be a brawl, a free-for-all, a riot, or a mugging, such as we encounter on our streets, and on byways that require heavy policing. Archaic or primitive structures and traditions, such as they are in a world taken over by Western institutions, cordon off opportunities for violence that the mobility and freedom of our urban and exurban societies experience routinely. In *Black Boy* Richard Wright tells his own story about having to leave "for the warmth of other suns" because he knows that in the Jim Crow South, he would either kill somebody or kill himself. In his classic coming-of-age novel, *Native Son*, he achieved wide acclaim for daring to narrate the fate of a black rapist and murderer in Chicago. His principle model was *Crime and Punishment*—in its murderous protagonist Wright discovered the lineaments of his fiction, and its techniques he adapted to his needs. Dostoevsky was telling him his story. Of course, there was the "influence" of Dreiser and Mencken, etc., but more importantly there is the Russian novelist's probing interrogation of violence in our world as a lens for Wright's own experience. Wright also wrote a book called *The Man Who Lived Underground*. Ralph Ellison's *Invisible Man* owes its defining trope to Dostoevsky; its narrator writes from the unseen, underground space housing the utilities of New York streets, and he emerges in the "Epilogue" to identify his violent resentments in his readers in the very last sentence of his novel: "Who knows but that, on lower frequencies, I speak for you?"—as if echoing Dostoevsky's underground narrator in his closing remarks to his imaginary audience : "For my part, I have merely carried to extremes in my life what you have not dared to carry even half-way, and in addition, you have mistaken your cowardice for commonsense and have comfort in that, deceiving yourselves" (240). That is a pretty good way of describing the imaginative excesses of much that is excellent in fiction, not as a matter of influences but of hard-won structural insights that *envelop* the reader, one by one. Instead of influence, we need to think of confluence.

A further illustration of this revelatory activity is to be

found among some untranslated pages from *Des choses cachées* (144–145) not included in *Things Hidden*. Against the "referential nihilism" prevailing in Girard's intellectual climate, he raises a question about "the period in the US which extends from the Civil war to the struggle for *civil rights.*" He invites a comparison between administrative documents with "certain works that present themselves as fiction, signed by an individual named William Faulkner": "On the subject of lynching published at the time, the official documents will certainly be silent. If our historian is sufficiently observing, he will not fail to perceive the secret of that society and be aware of signs that are almost imperceptible, but whose significance will be revealed by the novels of William Faulkner." Michael Gorra's probing exploration of Faulkner's work within the context of the Civil War and its aftermath in Jim Crow, fills out this picture of the Southern novelist's depiction of his culture, in which he portrays an endless reprise of this fraternal combat and the racial policies that ensued it. His work is authoritative on the war's mutigenerational consequences, which endure unresolved to this day.

Ruminating distraughtly on this heritage, Quentin

Compson reflects, "Maybe happen is never once but like ripples maybe on water after the pebble sinks" (Faulkner, 28).

This image conveys the sense of a pattern in history that resonates with Mark Twain's oft-repeated quip: "History does not repeat itself, but it rhymes." This is to say that different events and episodes display common structures and dynamics, as I have suggested by Sophocles's potential reading of psychoanalytic history and that Girard applies as "mimetic history" in his book on Clausewitz. Faulkner's polyphonic innovations—a term first applied to Dostoevsky's novels by Bakhtin—in his narratives are exercises of his acute and painful historical consciousness, as are his switchback chronologies. For her own imaginative fiction, the writer and scholar Saidiya Hartman proffers the useful expression "critical fabulation" in the *New Yorker* profile of her work (Okeowo, 48), with the understanding that an uncritical or mythic fabulation would come from the point of view of persecutors, of lynchers, which Faulkner, for instance, adroitly unravels in his short story "Dry September" (1931).

The formal devices of narrative technique are of a piece with an author's "discovery procedure," which is how Eric

Gans labels the major works of the Western canon, including the Bible. Girard's recourse to Scripture is congruent with his search for demonstrable truths about ourselves at a universal, that is, anthropological level, with human self-understanding being a goal of literary studies and of humanities education in general. Faulkner's explicit biblical references (*Absalom! Absalom!* and *Go Down Moses*) are not ornamental but essential to his hermeneutic activity. In Girard's readings of literary masterpieces, images, figures of speech, symbols, are not decorative; they are interpretive keys to understanding; they are not embellishments, they put flesh on the bones of our thinking. Esthetics and epistemics couple and merge with the ethical. Divinely inspired or not, that's revelation for you.

In his deft reading of Faulkner, Gorra quotes Yeats: "We make out of the quarrel with others rhetoric but of the quarrel with ourselves, poetry," and goes on to remark, "that is what Faulkner did in his own heart: fought it out within his own great books" as he interrogates his own culture, a somewhat spectral region for those outside it. The novelist's depiction of alternating perspectives from within and without events reverberates with Girard's discussion of oscillating views, exterior and interior, on a culture: "I agree on the necessity to view the system from within and from without" (7). That is also Faulkner's answer. And Dostoevsky's as well: His novels and short stories involve the competing energies of Russia's religious traditions amid the modernizing forces of an ever more secularizing Europe. Yeats's comment can also remind us of the famous "crucible of doubt" from which the novelist forged his fictions.

In the next paragraph after the item on literature as a special domain, Aubral objects against Girard's avowed "sociological" critique of "religion" that he does not take it on as a "Marxist sociologist. His violence is lived as transhistorical universal which has nothing to do with capitalism and the bourgeoisie." That is quite true, but Lucien Goldmann, the eminent Marxist sociologist who carried forward the work of Georg Lukàcs, was among the first to hail Girard's insights. And since then, among the many studies of this kind, I will cite François Cusset's *Le Déchaînement du monde: Logique nouvelle de la violence*. The "déchaînement" ("unleashing") is a play on the work of Marcel Gauchet's *Le Désenchantement du monde*, for which the title shows a debt to the sociology of

Max Weber, and in which he describes the ongoing process of secularization activated by Western religion's self-critical propensity; he views Christianity as the "religion of the exit from religion." What is "new," as Cusset's subtitle avers, is the all-embracing scope of his study, involving current economic, political, broadly sociological, and pedagogical institutions, in which he detects the working of sacrificial practices; he abbreviates his penetrating critique under the heading of our "monde violence," our "violence monde," the two nouns being in constant and ubiquitous apposition. Kyle Edward Haden's critique of nationalism as idolatry (false transcendence for mimeticians) relies as much on Marx's definition of ideology as "mystified consciousness" as it does on biblical insights and injunctions, all of which aligns with Girard's idea of "méconnaissance," misrecognition, at the origin of culture and its ongoing gestation. Maintaining that "Our true freedom lies in relationality" (49), Haden shows, for instance, how the Beatitudes deregulate hospitality (109–110). Even to this day, censure of Girard ignores the growing library devoted to his ideas; the archive is duly referenced in his Wikipedia entry. Perhaps this is preaching to the choir; my point is that Aubral's critique brings us back to fundamental questions raised by Girard's work, of which the alleged breaches, gaps, leaps, etc., are being filled in by scholars worldwide—who find in his insights a hermeneutic for their own research areas.

Doubtless exercised by Girard's free-ranging, academically "undisciplined" comparisons and correlations, Aubral rightly asserts that "he is not a philosopher," as if that charge detected a defining flaw. But this is rather to his credit, at least for those persuaded by Richard Rorty's often jocular contention that philosophers have pretty much succeeded in talking themselves out of a job in their rational and bottomless quest for an epistemology. Rorty's argument is partly enabled by Derrida's deconstructions of philosophy as crypto-theology, a critique that Girard hails in *Violence and the Sacred* as it "demonstrates in striking fashion a certain arbitrary violence of the philosophic process as it occurs in Plato" (297); it is a demonstration that Derrida thereafter undertook in readings of Hegel and Heidegger, among others, right up through speech act theory. In this discussion it appears that Girard is comfortable with the term "deconstruction" (for which I have supplied the more homely image of "decoding") to the extent that it applies to the Bible's relentless undoing project, its ongoing critique of sacrificial practices from the privileged point of view of their victims. At the conclusion of *Violence and the Sacred*, he expresses a very un-Parisian "confidence in language" that has been under assault by myriad and dazzling critiques of representation (Derrida, Lacan, Foucault, Deleuze), seeing the critiques to "declare that language is incapable of expressing truth" (316), critiques that seem unmindful of what philosophers identify as a performative contradiction.

Girard is not a philosopher; he is a thinker, which is a different order of business than our research specializations allow for. In this discussion, he describes his concept of culture as "Shakespearean." Our best playwrights are notoriously masters of relational imagination. We might as well label Girard's thinking as Dostoevskyan. Not incidentally, the Russian novelist headed his works with an epigraph from scripture; he clearly felt he was engaged in the work of biblical revelation. Over time I have written up Girard variously as Pascalian, as Melvillian, as Buñuelian, and as still others among the cultural assets of our literary capital. I strongly suspect that, upon further reflection and analysis, we could find Girard to be Faulknerian, as Faulkner's fiction is acutely attuned to the structures and misconstructions of desire and violence, where incest, unexplored in creative works since Sophocles, is a manifold trope for enforced couplings and mystified rivalries. As if reprising Girard's founding quote from Heraclitus—"War is the father and king of all: some it makes gods, and some men; some slaves and some free"— Gorra summarizes Faulkner's historical consciousness as follows: "In that South, the Confederacy stood as a fixed point, and the war became the still and violent center of time itself" (322). Imagine that.

References

Alison, James. "Girard's Anthropology vs. Cognitive Archaeology." In *Violence and the Sacred in the Near East: Girardian Conversations at Çatalhöyük*, edited by Ian Hodder, 188–208. New York: Cambridge University Press, 2019.

Aubral, Francois. "René Girard, La violence et le sacré," *Revue Les Cahiers du Chemin* 17 (February 2, 1973): 192–205.

Borch-Jacobsen, Mikkel. *Le Sujet freudien*. Paris: Flammarion, 1982.

Cusset, François. *Le Déchaînement du monde: Logique nouvelle de la violence*. Paris: La Découverte, 2018.

Dostoievsky, Fyodor. "Notes from the Underground." In *The Best Short Stories of Dostoievsky*. Translated by David Magarshack, 107–240. New York: Modern Library, 1955.

Faulkner, William. *Novels 1936–1940*. New York: Library of America, 1990.

Gans, Eric. *Signs of Paradox: Irony, Resentment, and Other Mimetic Structures*. Stanford, CA: Stanford University Press, 1997.

Girard, René. *Violence and the Sacred*. Translated by Patrick Gregory. Baltimore: John Hopkins University Press, 1977.

———. *Des Choses cachées depuis la fondation du monde*. Paris: Grasset, 1978.

Gorra, Michael. *The Saddest Words: William Faulkner's Civil War*. New York: Liveright, 2020.

Haden, Kyle Edward. *Embodied Idolatry: A Critique of Christian Nationalism*. New York: Lexington Books, 2020.

Okeowo, Alexis. "Secret Histories." *The New Yorker*, October 26, 2020.

Discussion with René Girard

I am very happy to be here and participate in this debate. I am grateful for your interest in *Violence and the Sacred* and for your genuinely critical approach, something rare and precious. Even misunderstandings that may occur here are useful to the extent that they help to clarify and correct controversial points and defects.

My book is intended to be systematic, but it includes a personal approach. Many things in its composition and the choice of examples are determined by that approach. Perhaps that is an initial cause of misunderstanding. I began with literature, which plays an important role especially in the first chapters. In a systematic account, we might do without that, not for any fundamental reasons, but because the prejudice about an absolute separation between literature and science remains very strong. I would like my book to be read not as an essay but as the elaboration and assay of a hypothesis concerning the origin, structure, and function of religion we designate as primitive. From Evans-Pritchard through Dumézil, everyone agrees these days in affirming that an attempt of this kind has no chance of succeeding. In the history of research in this matter, a unanimous agreement about the impossibility of achieving any such results is often proclaimed at the very moment when such a result is on the horizon.

Over the centuries ethnologists have been building a really impressive archive of resemblances and differences on religious phenomena, but without any common basis of interpretation. We are at a stage like that of chemistry before Lavoisier or of evolution before Darwin. Some people think there is no place in ethnology for grand unifying theories of the kind that have marked the entry of numerous disciplines into our scientific world. But the play of differences and similarities is emerging in a way that is at once so puzzling and so visibly systemic in this archive that it cannot fail to arouse curiosity. It is just the type of enigma that has attracted current reflection of a structuralist character, in the most general sense of the term.

Of course it is true that the efforts of a comprehensive global explanation, at the end of the nineteenth and the beginning of the twentieth centuries, have all failed, but I think it is not true that the track record is entirely negative. Any science that finally succeeds in getting established does not disdain its ancestors; rather, it discovers essential intuitions among them. It does not exclude them from an account that recognizes its continuities as well as its departures. In this elaboration, structuralism in the narrow sense appears to me as a kind of strategic retreat; it is important for the illusions it dissipates, for the distinctions its sets up, but ultimately sterile. I think structuralism shows very well where religion is not to be found while regrettably proceeding to its systematic elimination.

The opposition between myth and ritual as defined by Lévi-Strauss is not justified in my view. It tries to restrict what is undifferentiated to a kind of ritual ghetto, but I see it as ultimately one with religious thought; he opposes this to mythic thought, which creates differences and forecasts scientific thought. To pull this off, you have to exaggerate the role of what is undifferentiated in rituals to the point of seeing that only, and to minimize it on the contrary in myths to the point of not seeing it at all. In myths as in rituals, it is the erasure of differences, by a mystery that is never explained, that allows them to appear or reappear more distinctly than ever, reinforced and stabilized. It is this passage through undifferentiation, culminating typically in the violence of sacrifice, that is the midwife to myriad subdivisions among groups, different seasons, etc.

Even before culminating in bloody sacrifice, the process of ritual undifferentiation is redolent with violence. The turmoil and promiscuities of *festivals*, for example, are often accompanied by quarrels or battles that that are variously simulated or real. By their rhythmic symmetry, by everything about them, the warlike dances or simulations of combat often precede sacrifices and prepare them, as they are party to this universal process of violent undifferentiation.

Mythic and ritual undifferentiation appears to correspond to a threat of *real* dissolution, to the reality of great social crises. Although societies reproduce these crises in their rituals, for reasons that might be accessible to us, they have a horror of undifferentiated violence, which is as strong in structuralism as it is in modern thought altogether. Perhaps it is because of the same horror among us today that we refuse to award the least credit to primitive horror. We always take it to be imaginary. That attitude rejects a formidable mass of concordant evidence.

This does not warrant a return to traditional types of historical inquiry. Rather, we have to raise the question of cultural origins afresh, but this time beginning with the process of orderly structuring and in a perspective that is not religious or philosophical but sociological. We have to be open to the possibility of systematizing this development, at least partially, in terms of mythic and especially ritual evidence that we always put aside without scrutiny, supposing them a priori to be somehow "mystical."

In the mythic descriptions of chaos and undifferentiated violence, which always issue in re-differentiating sacrifices, there are elements that are far too widespread for us to deny that they are permanent features of the way in which cultural systems are torn apart and reestablished.

In the light of this evidence we can elaborate a theory of crisis, by which I mean a theory of violent reciprocity whereby cultural differences dissolve. At the paroxysm of this crisis, the substitution of one antagonist for all the others becomes more and more likely. The least polarization exerts a mimetic attraction, which becomes irresistible as the antagonisms multiply. In no time at all, the community can find itself once again unified against a victim that is in reality arbitrary but is unanimously perceived as responsible for the crisis, and that is forthwith massacred on that account.

If the essential cause of the crisis is antagonistic mimesis, which sets men up against one another, that collective violence constitutes grounds for a kind of resolution; it frees the antagonists from their reciprocal hatred; it actually brings peace.

The beneficiaries of this mechanism are obviously incapable of recognizing its sociological character. The effectiveness of collective violence will therefore be attributed to the victim itself: On the one hand the guilt of the victim will be confirmed, and on the other the killers will experience a wondrous gratitude. All the while seeming pernicious in that it was and could again be a source of disorder in the community, this victim becomes auspicious and beneficial inasmuch as, once expelled, it appears to watch over the community from without.

None of the forms of collective violence that we know of, such as lynching, pogroms, etc., can be seen to coincide with the type of crisis I am postulating here, since they are never covered up and erased by the addition of a properly religious meaning. We must not, therefore, minimize but rather underline the hypothetical character of what I am advancing. It is not to be judged on the basis of its immediate plausibility but on its explanatory power. We have just seen that this hypothesis can account for the double nature, pernicious and beneficent, of the sacred [*sacer*] and of all the notions of the same type. I believe it can also account for all the major enigmas posed by the diversity and the unity of myths and rituals.

If the community has really suffered from this crisis, it is going to try hard to perpetuate and reinforce the fragile peace which it suddenly enjoys. The members of the community are going to refrain forever from any contact with what has served as a pretext rather than the true reason for the violence of the crisis—from women who have been fought over, from certain kinds of food, from certain contentious spaces, etc. Anything that appears infected by violence automatically suggests the sacred victim and is made the object of a *prohibition* for harboring a contagious impurity.

From the collective transfer, then, a primary imperative arises, that of taboo, sometimes absurd in its further iterations but also quite real, being motivated in its primary principle, which is no more "phantasmatic" than the one forbidding someone who has been burned from evermore touching what has burned him.

The same desire to perpetuate peace must needs suggest a second kind of behavior. Since the killing of the victim has pulled men out of the crisis, it is logical to renew the killing if they wish to renew its beneficial effects, if, that is, they dread falling back into the crisis. They will even suppose that the abominable and blessed victim has allowed himself to be sacrificed or has sacrificed himself, or that they have only sacrificed an arbitrary victim to instruct men in the redemptive act.

In the effect of the unique victim, we find therefore an event whose possibilities are extraordinary concerning social origins. A causal account for the double compulsion of ritual and taboo on the one hand, and on the other for the "ambivalence" of the sacred emanating from one and the same mechanism, and thoroughly integrating them—this is a possibility not to be ignored. And I think we can show that the validity of the hypothesis remains intact when we go into the details of religious forms, as diverse as they only appear or as they really are. There are rituals that demand the *unanimity* of its participants; there are others that choose their victim at *random*, by ludic processes or ones that require some sort of ordeal; there are some that literally seek to transfer the "evil"—or rather the violence—onto the designated victim by methods that are naively material, to be sure, but always revealing. These are what we call "scapegoat" rituals. I think that this category has no true specificity; it is founded, like other traits I have just enumerated, on the observation and reproduction of a real aspect of the transfer mechanism. Even the "ritualism" of the rite reveals herein its soundness. Religious thought knows that it is ignorant of the mechanism it seeks to reproduce, so it tries hard to copy everything as exactly and completely as possible. That is why, incidentally, it must reproduce traits that belong not only to the resolution of the crisis but to the crisis as well—the two being inseparable—provoking thereby objective contradictions between the rituals and the prohibitions that the cultures at first and the anthropologists after them often endeavor to deny or minimize.

We need to rediscover the soundness of rituals, and follow religious observations without being governed by religious thinking. While not trusting it blindly, we have to refrain from the contrary prejudice according to which religious thought is something purely imaginary. We have to understand that even its affirmation of transcendence corresponds to a sociological reality. The community is aware that it is incapable of reconciliation on its own, as by some face-to-face social contract: that it cannot achieve reconciliation without victims. Men unite first against and then around their victims. The founding mechanism enables us to give a concrete content to Durkheim's intuition, as yet void of substance, about the identity of the religious and of the social, and not owing to some general idea but to a real collective mechanism. Between the founding event and concrete religious forms, there are always gaps, confusions, lacunae, owing to the inaccessible character of the truth, which is sociological. That margin of incertitude and of erroneous interpretation is itself foundational, giving rise on the one hand to innumerable differences among diverse religious forms, and on the other hand, and more essentially, giving rise to cultural Difference as such. Although it appears as the fruit of a double and unique, all-powerful intervention from the outside, the one intended to punish but not destroy men, the other to save them. The whole process constituted by the crisis and its resolution must be traced to the victim itself. I am saying that the social truth of violence is in a sense expelled along with the victim, outside the community and outside human culture altogether.

So it is not a question of forcing all religious forms into one standard mold. On the contrary, it is a question of explaining the diversity as well as the unity of these same forms by hypothesizing what they are aiming at without ever really succeeding. Think of it, if you will, as the irregular pattern of shots scattered around a target without ever hitting its center.

Undifferentiation or Inversion

Michel Panoff: First of all, I would like to talk about the problem of differentiation. As much as I agree with what you have said of your effort to build a bridge across the divide between ritual and myth as laid out by Lévi-Strauss, I am nonetheless uneasy about the use and meaning of this word undifferentiation in certain parts of your book.

René Girard: You are quite right, and I wonder if my use of this term is regrettable, because it gives the impression that the destruction of the difference that culture makes is the fundamental reality. Doubtless we should always keep talking about violent reciprocity.

Michel Panoff: One has the uncomfortable impression that at times it is undifferentiation that causes violence and at times it is violence that generates undifferentiation. We can just as well conceive of a circular process, which would solve the problem and answer my question. But as to the meaning of the word undifferentiation, I wish to insist: I have the impression that, concerning rituals, very often this word is used in a rather hazy manner. Because, when the examples that you give of undifferentiation are closely inspected, it seems that we're talking about inversion, and that's quite different. All folklores contain examples of the King of Carnival, and everyone here knows the famous day of inversion in the preparatory classes of the Grandes Ecoles on December 2, when older members are hazed by the new ones. There is no undifferentiation; the same rules are applied with all the roles reversed. It seems to me that the rituals that you cite as the demonstration and manifestation of undifferentiation belong to the category of inversion. So I have a certain uneasiness that I also encounter with Lévi-Strauss when he writes about binary oppositions.

René Girard: I will answer with a contemporary example. Let's take national conflicts. At the outset, one camp adopts a position on a problem, the other adopts the inverse of that. It is in the name of that difference, or if you will, that *differend*, that the conflict seeks its justification. After a while, it happens that the positions are reversed, the opposition remains but in a contrary direction. Then a moment arrives, and we are in one such a phase, where the inversions become so rapid and numerous that unless you yourself "committed," you can no longer take the differences seriously, no longer justify the conflict by them; it is the conflict, on the contrary, that multiplies ever more unstable differences. The meaning of the difference is vanishing, giving way to a violent reciprocity that is properly senseless. I believe that binary oppositions are as important and frequent as Lévi-Strauss thinks they are, because, behind the myths and rituals, there are violent crises where re-differentiation is achieved by the collective expulsion, by the effect of the unique victim. When there really is conflict, there are ever only two antagonists or two antagonistic factions. That is why we find so many binary oppositions in myths that are "badly differentiated," why we find sacred twins, for example, like Romulus and Remus.

Michel Panoff: Your answer is quite convincing, but it is not about rituals; all these situations are found outside of ritual.

René Girard: I think that rites attempt to reproduce the collective resolution, the saving and dedifferentiating effect of the unique victim. But this effect is situated at the paroxysm of the crisis. Consequently, rites pose problems for disjunction that are resolved in various ways in religious thinking. In certain rites, such as rites of passage, or festivals, the entire crisis will be mimicked because it is remembered as the necessary prelude to expulsion, which is the condition of its effectiveness. In the rite you will find inversions that are increasingly rapid, then at the paroxysm, a blurring of differences that culminates in phenomena like possession, as I see it. You find at once increasingly rapid inversions that culminate in a *monstrosity* (at the moment when everything appears to be simultaneous), and also *doubles*, because everything is always the same on one side as on the other.

If you read the descriptions of sacrificial "preparations," you note that ethnologists talk sometimes of "simulated combat," of "warlike dancing," or quite simply of dance and song. As long as we conceive the relation as combat, we don't see the symmetry and even the perfect identity of gestures, of tactical maneuvers, of feints, and of course of selfsame objectives on the one side as on the other. Nevertheless, each one responds to the offensive gesture of the other by a defensive gesture *reproducing* it but not yet conceived as copying, imitation. From the moment when, in the rite, the antagonism disappears, being replaced by the effective collaboration of a mimo-drama, nondifference becomes manifest, and the combat is transformed into a rhythmic dance.

In the light of this, I think we can understand why Plato takes dance as the most mimetic of all the arts, which has always intrigued estheticians because they ever only see mimesis as pure representation, in the sense of the painter who wishes to "create a semblance." Dance is mimetic because it is essentially a relation of gestural imitation of two people who are face to face, as in a mirror.

In the phenomena of rites and dances we have no end of inversions that are experienced as differences. Masques are a combination of differences; they suggest the experience of one antagonist facing another antagonist, but it is most often a mask facing another mask; or in certain cultures, the mask itself is divided into two, as you know; but in the rite itself you will find inversions and in any event you will always find an underlying symmetry, reciprocity.

Michel Panoff: Yes, but I have the impression that precisely to the extent that you have inversion, you have at the same time the affirmation or reaffirmation of difference. That is clearly the case with royal incest.

René Girard: But of course, since by definition all rites and all myths are situated and define themselves in relation to the results of the process, therefore in relation to a sacred that is already in existence, in relation to a victim who is differentiated from the rest; everything is always recuperated as difference.

Michel Panoff: Yes, but to that extent you cannot put in an equal sign or any sort of inclination between the undifferentiation of real violence that you want to expunge and the undifferentiation that you are examining in your book when you write about inversions that are practiced in rituals.

René Girard: We have to conceive how, although invisible to antagonists, the nondifference of the relation is effective on the level of the collective transfer before it becomes manifest in the rite, at the very heart of the crisis. That is what assures the transfer of reciprocal aggressions onto any member of the group. For those who live the experience from within it, there are only differences, which are unstable and oscillating in the crisis, and stabilized by the expulsion. Nondifference, that is to say, the reciprocity of actual relations, ever only makes its appearance later on, in the symmetry of ritual dancing, or more elusively in the mythic *doubles* who are always somewhat redifferentiated, reprised with meaning.

To this day no one sees *doubles* as an actual relation of antagonism that is nonsignificant, that is pure violent reciprocity. Structural linguistics can only understand dual oppositions as significant and differentiated; psychoanalysis only sees *doubles* as an imaginary phantom of the subject.

Pierre Pachet: This point interests me as having to do with a thorny question of vocabulary that I think causes some difficulty with Girard's thinking. It's about the word "undifferentiated." When we talk about differences and differentiation, we either think of a couple or a system of marks; as a result, undifferentiation brings to mind a field characterized by the imaginary, the illogical, by elasticity and flow, a field outside or on the other side of anything systematic. This is how certain myths appear to work: before there was chaos, the biblical tohu-bohu; then order sets in. Contrary to this, Girard's thought unveils a logical framework of the undifferentiated while giving it tangible content: the undifferentiated, which always eludes straightforward comprehension, is not a mark; it's just the opposite. It nonetheless shows up at the moment when a couple of terms are perceived as couples of doubles (whence the importance of the universal theme of twins). This is especially the case at the moment we can only postulate when all thinkable differences in a system begin to circulate wildly in search of a fixed boundary that has disappeared. Undifferentiation would not be a state within a system but a moment of tension, of oscillating equilibrium, and so of disequilibrium.

Michel Panoff: Fine, but linguists are familiar with this sort of problem. When they talk about difference, about opposition, it is by contrast with another notion, that of neutralization, and this has nothing to do with what I find in rituals and that Girard presents as a process of undifferentiation.

Pierre Pachet: I agree with you: In linguistics the possibility of neutralization exists; it is even fundamental. But nothing allows us to suppose that, when dealing with conflicts where the entire social system is at stake, neutralization is the right notion. Girard proposes another idea that he calls undifferentiation. Of course, this is a term that can mean too much or too little, but it leads to something. It signifies that a certain state of a system can be seen in two ways: Seen from within the system, it is difference; seen from without, it is inversion. But I don't think the word inversion describes it much better: It functions as if there were only an exterior point of view—whereas what is undifferentiated concerns a point of view oscillating between the interior and exterior, rather like what Girard would call as a disenchanted snob.

René Girard: I agree on the necessity to view the system from within and from without. But it seems to me that we can speak of undifferentiation at the paroxysm of violent relations, quite simply because the very rapidity of reprisals, the *feedback loop* of violence, excludes any stable, perceptible difference. I think that is what the Greek tragedians mean when they describe the death of Eteocles and Polyneices. It is impossible either to affirm or deny anything about one of the two brothers without having to affirm or deny it about the other. The whole problem of interminable violence is there. It is why Creon thinks he can differentiate between the enemy brothers; but it is striking to notice that in his first speech in *Antigone*, he comes up with an expression that is analogous to the ones you find in Aeschylus in *Seven against Thebes* and in Euripides that specifically state the impossibility to distinguish between them:

Creon: "In their double destiny the two brothers perished on the same day, giving and receiving blows foul blows." Euripides, in *The Phoenician Women*, concludes his description of the combat thus: "With dust in their teeth, each the murderer of the other, they lie side by side, and the power is not shared between them."

It is the same problem, in my view, that we find everywhere, and especially in Isaac's benediction of Jacob. The astute substitution of one brother for another clearly reveals how ending the crisis consists in stabilizing difference by the unanimous expulsion of one of the *doubles*; it does not matter which one. As I see it, ritual consists in reliving all these moments successively: inversion first, with increasing rapidity, the actual undifferentiation of *doubles*, and finally sudden redifferentiation, thanks to sacrifice. But nothing of that sort appears in myths, which are always papered over by a significant difference. In ritual this is a bit more clear.

Even the Seasons Are Disturbed

Michel Panoff: Fine, but when you talk about ritual as a substitution or remedy for vendetta, it is because rituals provide something other than vendetta. When we discuss differentiation and inversion you answer with vendetta, but this violence is different. I spent two years in New Guinea and it is different. The Maenge of New Brittany where I lived had vendettas that fairly resembled what you call undifferentiation, but they also had rituals where you find inversions, binary oppositions, etc. So I have the impression that if we continue along this route, the debate that began between myth analysis in Lévi-Strauss and ritual analysis in Girard is not viable, because this debate bears on two symbolic processes, while vendetta is a reality that is not yet symbolized.

René Girard: If ritual, according to you, is a substitute for vendetta, it is because it concerns something else than vendetta. I agree. But this something else that ritual provides is the *imitation* of the collective phenomenon that had long ago resolved the problem of vendetta, by the unanimous transfer of violence on the unique victim. Since that resolution springs up from the paroxysm of a similar crisis, the ritual can indeed decide on the need to reproduce the paroxysm and even the entire crisis. That is why ritual always has something paradoxical about it. You have to get men to relive, as a simulacrum but nonetheless close enough, the very thing that they seek to avoid or whose return they seek to prevent. If the rite does that, it is meant to lead once again—and this is what we fail to see—to the kind of resolution by means of a sacrifice that proved effective the first time.

Some observers have argued, and I think they are right, for the psycho-sociological effectiveness of the rite. They discern the real function of the rite, but I think they are mistaken if they think that that real function suffices to justify the existence of the rite, if they think that no supplementary explanation is necessary. How do we explain what takes place in the rite? My hypothesis explains at once its function and its origin: The rite is the weakened reproduction of the original *catharsis*. If the community is once again plagued by violence, it fears falling back into violence, it makes sense to have recourse to a remedy that cured them a first time, even if this remedy is situated at the very heart of the evil that men seek to evade.

Michel Panoff: The unity of all rites is the problem. That is the title of your last chapter in *Violence and the Sacred*. I am convinced by your analysis of rites of passage; I think that in fact we can trace them all back to your model, but what about rites of fertility, rites for building a cultic edifice, for dwelling places, etc., where we don't see any victims? I could go into detail about rites in the cultures that I have studied.

René Girard: There are a great number of founding rites that consist in burying a sacrificial victim in the groundwork of an edifice under construction. I have tried to show that the sacred king, for example, is at the start only a victim like any other, a victim of the sacrificial process. I am trying to show that the major rites, however different later on, can be traced back to a common origin.

As for fertility rites and in general all the rites where nature is implicated, I think that there is a projection of the social model onto phenomena that are not unrelated to the extent that they bring into play human activities, such as labor. Concord among farmers is no less important for the harvest than rain and sun, which also have a capricious character, even though less capricious than human relations. So we can understand how sacrifice and rituals can be imagined to influence the elements.

Michel Panoff: Fine, but all that is hugely mediated. I raise this question because it allows us to discern, in a religious totality that you abbreviate as primitive religion, all sorts of aspects and elements that really have no great relation to violence.

René Girard: Perhaps so, but this mediated dimension is an integral part of my hypothesis. Violence is expelled from the community, out into nature consequently, and it is normal that nature play a prominent role. The sacred, as I see it, is everything that weighs down on men from outside their control, for good or ill. As of the moment when what is essential, which concerns the relations among humans within their community, is projected outward, it can only appear in a garb that is not fallacious, since external threats really exist. Obviously, I am reversing the current perspective, which sees in religion an "anthropomorphism" of natural forces.

To find something analogous to what I am saying, we have to go back to Shakespeare, who can rarely dispense, in his dramas and comedies, with a whole orchestration of plagues and storms, of natural and cosmic catastrophes, so much so that commentators affirm sometimes that it is natural disorder that dominates and determines the disorders in human relations; but Shakespeare never fails to warn us that none of this is the case. In *A Midsummer Night's Dream*, for example, the context is the folkloric festival with inversions and confusions of all natural differences. Even the seasons are troubled, and we cannot tell summer from winter, fall from spring. You might think that the quarrels among the characters are only the reflection of this natural and cosmic chaos, but Titania ends her description of all this by reestablishing the true Shakespearean order when she affirms that it is her own conflict with Oberon that is essential. Here I think we find intuitions about festivals from which ethnologists might profit:

. . . The Spring, the summer,
The childing autumn, angry winter, change
Their wonted liveries; and the mazed world,
By their increase, now knows not which is which.
And this same progeny of evils comes from
Our debate, from our dissension; We
Are their parents and original. [2.1]

Oedipus or Mimetic Rivalry

Eugénie Luccioni: Mimesis seems to oppose two terms: let's say, a subject and a model; the roles can be reversed but there are still two terms and there is no reason for that to end; it can go on infinitely because we are in the realm of the ideal image. I am talking from Freud's point of view, whom you criticize, to postulate that the primary identification would perhaps be more manageable and more fertile because it postulates three terms and allows us to quit the imaginary and go to the level of the symbolic. The *mimesis* that you describe, for example, would be what Freud erroneously called identification in *Group Psychology and the Analysis of the Ego*. He describes Hitler's followers as everyone identifying with an image and everyone becoming the same. But that is not properly speaking identification, which is summed up perhaps in a typical game of "*fort, da, fort, da*" ["gone"/"there"]: A child of a few months holds a spool at the end of a thread, then throws it out of the crib and cries, "*Fort, da, fort, da.*" In this game, it imagines that the spool is his mother; it imagines that there is something that withholds or attracts the spool outside; that can be, at certain moments, the father or some voice that pulls the spool away; but it is also himself, since he deprives himself of the spool; it can be everyone successively. There is a play of substitution that is precisely one of the laws of symbolic language.

René Girard: You say *mimesis* poses two terms, and that there is no reason for that to end, that it can go on infinitely because we are in the realm of the ideal image. But for me this is not at all about an ideal image, but of real conflict among real humans. And there is actually a reason in my view for that to end, a reason *that belongs to no one;* that is why it is soon going to pass for transcendental. That reason is the collective transfer onto the unique victim that transforms conflictual *mimesis* into unifying *mimesis.* It is through this mechanism, rooted in *mimesis,* that I see the emergence of what Durkheim calls social transcendence and that Lacan, if I understand him, sometimes calls the *symbolic,* rightly asserting its fundamental character. I see the emergence of all that from mimetic desire as it leads to the collective transfer.

Eugénie Luccioni: But how?

René Girard: In Lacan, if I understand him, and I am not always sure I do, the *symbolic* is always already there; if it is lacking, you have psychotic "forclusion." From a Lacanian perspective, my work must be read not as stagnation in the imaginary—the favorite rebuke of his school—but as a foolhardy effort to resolve the problem of origins, of differentiating capabilities, and of the historical disintegration of the symbolic.

As I see it, it is a mistake to approach problems by starting out with psychoanalytic theories, some of whose postulates do not appear well founded and in any event will always remain too fixed within synchronic boundaries.

Far from situating myself in the imaginary because *mimesis* is my starting point, it is the third term that interests me the most, but my conception of it is more Empedoclean, so to speak, or more Shakespearean, than Lacanian.[1]

Eugénie Luccioni: When the infant sees itself in the mirror—an infant or an adult if there is no third term—it is confused with its double. The infant does not even see it; it is the third term that enables the play, I mean the gap between doubles. There is no other possibility.

René Girard: I do not believe in the "mirror stage" of child development. It strikes me as an impasse, a perpetuation of the solipsism that characterizes the Freudian notion of narcissism, and that of Otto Rank in *The Double and Don Juan.* They always talk about the *double* from the point of view of the individual subject, seeing it as a phantom, a phantasm, or imaginary, instead of the point of view on two people, that is to say, in tangible relations. I think this is important for a critique of the philosophical foundations of psychoanalysis, which never take a view of relations but only of the isolated subject.

Eugénie Luccioni: If you don't postulate the issue as three, you cannot even pose it as two, because the one and the other are confused.

René Girard: As you wish; I won't refuse your third term.

Eugénie Luccioni: I will give a more precise example. You say the son would not desire his mother if he were not imitating his father, who already desires her. You prefer to explain everything in terms of imitation, which is violent, even regarding the desire for the mother, rather than admit that the desire is also perhaps primordial.

René Girard: I find that thinking about desire has for a century tended to detach it from any mooring in objects, and that Nietzsche, for example, goes farther in this direction than Freud, who holds on to one and only object, but an absolutely privileged object, the mother. This trend uprooting the object seems right because it leads us gradually to understand that desire is governed not by objects but by *others*. To follow through with this idea is to understand that the essential conflict is the one with the mimetic model. This conflictual mechanism, which Freud seems to have missed because he didn't want to let go of his Oedipus complex, has an extreme simplicity about it, but it is so rich with possibilities for understanding relations among humans that I necessarily find it preferable to the Oedipus complex. I see no more in the Oedipus complex than a more or less mythical variant, inappropriate and ossified, of the same mechanism.

Eugénie Luccioni: That does not make it more scientific.

René Girard: What is scientifically decisive, ultimately, is the ability of a hypothesis to organize the data that it gathers and to account for them. Some think that they have in psychoanalysis an instrument that is effective for ethnological interpretation. Perhaps they are not exacting enough.

Let us suppose, for example, that I accept the Oedipus complex. I can delude myself about its explanatory power as long as I consider only one type of phenomenon at a time. In certain cultures, for example, the prohibition of incest suffers no exception. That works easily for this complex. In other cultures, incest is not only tolerated but required, either by certain exceptional individuals, or by all the members of the community at certain festivals. That too works easily for the complex. In most cultures elderly people are not only respected but there is an effort to prolong their life as much as possible. That too works for the complex. In other cultures, it happens that old people are done away with; among the Dinka, for example, they do not want their *spear masters*, the most prestigious among the old, to die a natural death. That works for the complex. But psychoanalysis never tells me why this universal Oedipal *mana* is specified in such different ways in different cultures. Let us suppose I know nothing about railroad technology; I observe the maneuvers in the station; I see cars moving to the right and I see some going to the left. I will never understand what is going on unless I have a hypothesis that will give me, *grosso modo*, a theory of *junction boxes*. Don't tell me that the libido of the locomotive, even canalized in Oedipal tubing, is a sufficient explanation for all this. I never see, in psychoanalytic theory, the junction boxes that would explain why one culture takes off on rails to the right and another on ones to the left. And I am taking examples that are particularly favorable to psychoanalysis since we are concerned with the presence or absence of *incest* and *murder of the fathers*.

Perhaps I am mistaken, but I think that my hypothesis of collective transfer onto a unique victim, as weighty as it appears to some, gives me the junction boxes that are lacking in psychoanalysis. Incest is the destruction of family order, it is undifferentiating and undifferentiated violence. It is therefore understandable that it is prohibited. But the sacred king incarnates the victim: he must first polarize malefaction in order to expel it in sacrifice; it is therefore understandable that incest, among other transgressions, is demanded of him. By the same token, it is understandable that the entire culture gives itself over to incest in festivals that reproduce the ensemble of the crisis and its resolution, in order to renew the benefits of the latter. By the same token, it is understandable that the warrior who is going off to battle commits incest so as to somehow imbibe a violence that would be disastrous within the community but will be useful against enemies.

Eugénie Luccioni: But your assertion—the son only desires his mother because his father desires her—strikes me as gratuitous.

René Girard: That assertion has in fact no meaning in itself. What I mean is that if there is anything to the Freudian Oedipus complex, it is a particular and mythified case of mimetic rivalry. In that case, the desire for the mother comes from the father. But I do not at all admit a primal desire for the mother, regardless of what form it takes. I even think that it is the most sensational mystification in modern thought.

I've noticed that Freud's first definitions of the Oedipus complex give a sense of mimetic rivalry, because they insist on identification with the father, on the desire to replace the father. In my analyses, I have tried to show that when Freud realized that this identification with the father threatened to disintegrate his Oedipal complex, he eliminated the expressions that tended to base desire for the mother on identification with the father.

The Tragedy of History

Jean-Marie Domenach: Let's move on to some questions about tragedy that I will present piecemeal. When this is in focus, there is fundamental criticism of your ambiguity regarding our historical situation. A moment ago you said something that interests me, namely, how to place ourselves in the history of culture. But then I wonder if the tragedy you discuss is situated in history or if it is an archetype, as you seem to suggest when you award it the interpretive privilege in the way that you do. If the tragedy is in history, then it signifies other things that the historians teach us; and, with particular regard to sacrifice, it is not only about killing but also about consuming. As Vidal-Naquet has pointed out, tragedy was not only tied to a sacrificial crisis, one that does not seem to have existed when tragedy made its appearance in history; but it was tied even more to the social and cultural situation of certain groups in the Polis who were engaged in a critique of its fundamental beliefs. I myself would go as far as to say that the history you explain so well is our own history, that of deritualized consumption. But your analysis does not seem to apply very well to history prior to us; it does not, for example, hold together at all for the era of the great barbarian invasions. And when you argue for sacrificial crisis as the essential key for interpretation, I have the sense of something that works as an invaluable interpretation both for proto-historical or primitive cultures and for the period we are living; but it is not helpful as an overall vision of history. Here I am going back to my question about tragedy as archetype. As I read you, I end up wondering if you are fixated overmuch on an origin, which leads you, in spite of your remarks on cultural paleontology, to repudiate any notion of progress, and even of evolution, and to suggest instead an eternal return.

René Girard: In my view, tragedy is not an archetype; it is the beginning of a "deconstruction" of religion, of the revelation of violence. I see the implicit contradiction that you point out. In my book, I am trying to develop a theory of primitive religions, and it is circular. But to describe what I call *sacrificial crisis*, namely, a moment in that circular theory, I am using texts that speak of that crisis, the pre-Socratics, the tragedians, because they themselves are informed by it. But it could not have been just a sacrificial crisis "like all the others." Neither do the fifth-century Greeks nor the sixteenth-century English lead up to a new ritual system in the narrow sense.

We are no longer in the narrow circle of primitive religion where the least violent rivalry, the least competition, can dissolve then rebuild ritual rigidities; these circles are infinitely wider, or rather we have a series of ever-widening circles with temporary regressions, such as, perhaps, in the high Middle Ages. And it is when we pass from one circle to another that that these crises resemble sacrificial crises, but in a strict sense they are not such since they almost always open up onto a system involving more substitutions and more competition, and so they are less narrowly sacrificial than the one preceding it. Our world is characterized by institutions that are doubtless born of ritual, but are always more differentiated: our judicial system first, but also politics in general, secular culture, the division of labor, the monetary system, etc. Without that ever-growing freedom with regard to violence, there would not even be a discourse about violence or about myths. But where does that freedom come from? Does it mean that we have definitively escaped from violence? These are problems that the questions posed earlier about Judeo-Christianity allow us to address.

Social Conflict and Social Contract

Michel Deguy: An objection comes to me as I listen to Domenach, who seems to suppose that Girard's thesis would be more generally true for our historical epoch. Could we not say the opposite? I wonder if it is not simply the case that all social strife is differentiating. Does not the history of the last 150 or 200 years show that at bottom social strife genuinely concerns groups struggling to be recognized in their differences. To put it another way, far from postulating the massive kind of equation: violence equals undifferentiation, perhaps we can read certain historical periods, in particular the most recent, as periods where conflict and violence are differentiating because they express the effort of groups that have been ignored to have their "true" differences recognized. Social progress is caught up in struggle and violence, but it cannot be interpreted as a presacrificial state of mind leading to undifferentiation.

René Girard: The massive equation you mention is only true, precisely, for societies we call "primitive," that is to say, lacking a judicial system and other institutions relatively more effective against violence than ritual, though they are born of ritual. I am only speaking here of differences that a culture values and that conceal the reciprocity among humans, which, by that very fact, by a reversal that is easy to understand, can serve as a struggle *for reciprocity*. When African Americans adhere to their blackness, when Italian

Americans their Italianness, I do not believe that this movement corresponds to the affirmation of real differences; I think to the contrary that they constitute a movement toward integration into modern society.

Michel Deguy: What bothers me is the devaluation of all social struggles.

René Girard: Absolutely not. That paradox is that reciprocity is only perfected by extremes of violence or nonviolence. Until today, humans have never been able to come up with the latter; they have always camouflaged and mutilated reciprocal exchanges by cultural differences, the minimum of nonviolent reciprocity that they cannot do without. Every time reciprocity shatters the screen of cultural differences in societies we call primitive, it takes the form of unbridled competition that degenerates into violent reciprocity. That is what explains the primitive terror of reciprocity, which is always perceived as violent undifferentiation. To understand that this terror is not groundless, to understand that we have not, to this day, been able to do without cultural differences and sacrifice—that is not at all to repudiate contemporary efforts, but rather measure their true worth. This leads us to a better understanding of the unprecedented originality of the modern demand for reciprocity, its universal significance and the difficulties it must needs encounter; it leads us to situate all that in relation to its genuine *other*, namely, a universal way of living; sacrifice is the route from which we wish to wrest ourselves completely, but the very violence of the exertion causes us to fall back into violence, because sacrifice is one with violence.

Paul Thibaud: I would like to know how what you have just said, considering the possibility of overcoming the sacred and its violence, goes along with your constant refutation of the notion of the social contract.

René Girard: Until now there have been, explicitly or implicitly, only two concepts of origins: religious origins that camouflage violence, projecting it, at least partially, onto the divinity, and the social contract that completely denies that same violence. Freud himself falls back inevitably upon the social contract even in *Totem and Taboo*, which is to say, the work that comes closest to showing the foundational role of the unique victim. Instead of explaining cultural integration from murder, Freud explains the murder as the result of tensions produced by culture or by preculture, which comes to the same thing. Consequently, he too is bound to have recourse to some kind of social contract to account for the prohibition of incest. He says that the brothers, to avoid conflict, have to agree among themselves to abjure certain women. So there is for Freud, as there is for Lévi-Strauss, an anti-incest social contract that strikes me as utterly implausible.

It seems to me that this insuperable recourse to the social contract is a major obstacle to anthropological understanding; it is one with the failure to attribute any real function to religion, the failure to acknowledge that it has protected humans up to now from our own violence by at once dressing it up as a transcendent bogeyman and by providing the permissible routes through sacrifice to prevent self-destruction. Moreover, this is why every traditional religion causes a scandal when it disintegrates; the violence that is in it loses its protective character and becomes pure and simple violence. This is what is happening today to all the remaining historical forms of religion, including Christianity. And this disintegration today is more radical than it has ever been, simply because it is no longer possible to expel violence by violence. We see this every day. Technology gives such powerful means to violence that men step back from using it. That is why the temptation of despair is everywhere present, now that the terrifying possibilities of human violence are fully revealed.

Nonetheless, it seems to me that the temptation to despair is not justified. What appears to justify it is the illusion of a nonviolent origin entertained first by religious thought and thereafter by postreligious thought, such as the social contract. If humans, from the very beginning, have been capable of getting along with one another rationally, been capable of mutual affection, of enlightened self-interest, how have we arrived at the point where we are today? If, to the contrary, we understand that there never has been a social contract, that humans have never turned aside from destroying one another without being held together by a sacred terror and the sacrificial deviations of violence, we then understand that what is happening today, as terrible as it is, has a positive signification. For the first time, humans pull back from violence without relying on a false transcendence, because we see its disastrous consequences. Thanks to science, we have maneuvered into this extraordinary position that no longer leaves any choice between two forms of absolute reciprocity, violence and nonviolence; of total annihilation or "utopia," the doorway to a world that will no longer be sacrificial nor even cultural in the sense that we lend to this term.

Jean-Marie Domenach: But then, if humans find ourselves faced with naked violence, we are at the moment of the great mediator, truly the moment of revelation.

René Girard: Far from plunging us into peevish delight [*delectatio morosa*] or a paranoid persecution complex, I find the revelation of our violent origin and of the violence of culture to be compelling not only on the scientific level, but, for the first time, helpful on the existential and social level. It should dispel the positivist illusion of automatic progress borne on the wings of a providential science, as well as the contrary and twin illusion we fall into these days of the absurd, of nonknowledge, and of utter heterogeneity; the belief that there is no such thing as universal history and that our human adventure is bound to fall back into nonsense. Nonsense certainly appears within our grasp, since we can at any moment end everything, but if we don't do it—and we have not done it yet—what we are facing is certainly not "relativizable" or tainted with "ethnocentrism."

The Sociological Explanation of Religious Thinking

Maurice Mourier: A moment ago you said we must not confuse the mechanism of the emissary victim with collective murders that can take place after great catastrophes. But in reading your book, it seems to me that we can consider the emissary victim as potentially a collective being. I was thinking, for example, of Nazism, which isn't very far back, and thinking of how easily we tend to read Jewish genocide as a phenomenon of emissary victimage. I would like to know if you would reject that idea.

René Girard: Rather than "mechanism of the emissary victim," the expression I use in *Violence and the Sacred*, I now prefer, "the effect of collective transfer on an arbitrary victim"; this is perhaps less equivocal because it is free of any ritual connotations. "Scapegoat" has wide currency, especially since Frazer, I suppose, to designate all the rites that consciously aim at reproducing an effect of collective transfer onto a sacrificial victim, a stand-in for the original victim. These rites are especially revealing as they are based on an altogether remarkable observation of the mechanism they aim to reproduce. That does not mean that we have to place them in a special category nor to view the Hebrew "scapegoat" ritual of Leviticus in a special category. We can just as well speak of the Greek *pharmakos* rites or yet another rite to designate a category that has, I repeat, no other specificity than the representation and repetition in a massive form of the mechanism of collective transfer. What determines the category is first of all ritual thinking that may or may not observe, may or not concretize what results from the transfer and, second, what is thereafter available to our observation, ethnological observation, that in turn may or may not detect these concretizations.

On the other hand, we must note that the expression "scapegoat" and its equivalents in other Western languages are used to designate both ritual forms and, paradoxically, spontaneous phenomena, notably in the case of frenzied crowds. "Scapegoat" is equally used for a whole gamut of intermediate forms between what is entirely ritual and what is entirely spontaneous. Given the difference, radical for some, between what is *ritual* and what is *spontaneous*, the variegated usage of "scapegoat" raises a host of issues that my research seeks especially to elucidate. So my answer to your question is necessarily "yes." But my immediate assent does not clarify any of the formidable problems posed by the historical specificity of the phenomenon that you bring up in the world that we have made for ourselves.

Maurice Mourier: A moment ago what you said about neo-Darwinism, and the nonpejorative sense you lend to the word "positivism," exhibit a frame of mind, an ideology, that underlies your book and seems based on the refusal, or the elimination, of any notion of transcendence. Your explanation of rituals and myths is one centered on man as a biological being; it is as if this being were led to create myths of transcendence at the endpoint of his thought as the result of a necessary process of biological development.

Is this not a radically materialist and atheistic theory of the origin of myths and rituals? I would like to know if you accept this way of reading your book.

René Girard: That reading of *Violence and the Sacred* is correct. Its primary aim is to provide a radically sociological explanation of religious thought, to show that in our twofold conception of what we call the "ambivalence" of the sacred, we are in fact dealing with a transfiguration of human violence that was for a long time necessary to the survival and development of humanity and that in our time is outdated, finished, whether or not we destroy ourselves as a consequence of the present crisis.

The Astounding Effectiveness of Christianity

As we examine our present situation, we have to ask what role can religion—our religion this time, Judeo-Christianity—play in this strange order of things. It is accused at times of perpetuating sacred terror, at times, with Toynbee, of opening up the route to scientific investigation and technological development, and therefore ultimately of not dispensing enough sacred terror.

The gospels situate themselves explicitly at the paroxysm of a crisis, one that John the Baptist defines as sacrificial and in line with the prophecies that we find at the beginning of Second Isaiah: all the valleys shall be filled, "*all the mountains lowered*" [Isa 40:4]. It is the great tragic leveling, the triumph of reciprocal violence. That is why the mutual recognition between John the Baptist and Christ, which is to be taken as prophetic and messianic authentication, is utterly devoid of antagonistic symmetry; it is the simple and miraculous fact of not succumbing to the vertiginous effect of violence.

To speak of paroxysm here is to recognize that the crisis can at any moment lead to the collective transfer and the sacred victim. The condemnation and death of Christ clearly bear collective markings. So it can seem to many that all is in due order, that Christianity is exactly the same thing as all other religions, a reiteration of the same mythico-ritual mechanism that we find everywhere else. That is what rationalist and anti-Christian thought has been repeating for centuries. Our enormous religious encyclopedia has been built up to demonstrate that identity. What has been driving the enterprise is the refutation of Christianity, and it would seem that the revelation of the founding mechanism is the last nail in the coffin.

In fact, nowhere is this mechanism more visible than in the gospels. At this point such solid evidence collapses into its opposite. If Christianity is a religion like all the others, that violent origin would be no more visible than in the others. Of course one could rejoin, saying I have misinterpreted; I am manipulating the texts. But that is impossible in this case; everything is written down in black and white in all four gospels. For the violent foundation to be effective, it must remain hidden; here it is completely revealed.

As soon as we discern this imperceptible but fundamental reversal, myriad enigmatic texts become clear and a new logic imposes itself; scattered elements recombine and spell out a coherent whole. When Christ says to his listeners *"you have killed all the prophets"* [Mt 23.29ff], there is no "antisemitism" here, as Freud avers in *Moses and Monotheism*. But these words are more comprehensive and they go much farther because they appear in a context that is otherwise significant.

The prophet is the one whose death generates our religious thinking, which is invariably founded on a collective murder. The same is true for our judicial system and our politics. When the High Priest Caiaphas affirms "*it is better that one man die for the people than that the nation be destroyed*" [Jn 11:38], he is saying something that no sound and humane politics could disavow, but he is also, without knowing it, spelling out the founding mechanism of all culture.

If this is the case, if we have this revelation, it is because Christ compels violence to reveal its game by refusing to have any part in it. We must not see in Christ what we find everywhere else, namely, the mythic reflection of a collective transfer that has a structuring role as long as it doesn't appear. We have to see in Christ the mysterious subject of this text who compels violence to inscribe itself in his person, forces it to come out in the open, to objectify itself so as to become gradually inoperative.

But, you will say, what about the resurrection? Isn't that once more the eternal game of sacralization, the death that comes out of life and the life that comes out of death? That is true only in appearance. Simone Weil saw this clearly; she described the "*Eloi, Eloi, lama sabacthani*" [Mk 15.34: "My God, my God, why have you forsaken me?"] as one of those utterances that make of the gospels a founding charter that is wholly unlike any others. Not so long ago those words either upset or delighted the doubling and innocent simplicity of our theologians and humanists, according to which side they were on; these words are decisive in just this, that they make of the death of Christ the same thing as our death, a death that is completely separated from resurrection and with no relation to it. Christ does not play with life and death in the manner of the phoenix, of the Aztec gods, or Dionysus.

All modern thought, from an increasingly Hellenized Christianity through deism and atheism, imagines that to make a big deal of unpleasant phenomena of the "scapegoat" type, and even worse to portray victims of it, is to fall back into ancestral superstitions. We always think we are free of ancient thralldom by erasing any question of origins, while in fact that erasure is one with the perpetuation of violent origins. We deal with gospel texts as colonizers did with the subject peoples, or as the respectable Americans from the South who thought they could erase one hundred years of lynching by never making the least allusion to it. The only text that truly reveals our violent origins has come to pass for the last one to fall to its control. Having sought to "purify" Christianity, to "cleanse" it of its "superstitions," we end up by expelling it entirely. In matters essential to us, our thought continues to function according to the primitive schema of contagious impurity.

We are dealing with a peremptory closure that has repercussions at every level. We do not see that the gospel texts always function as the revelation of all the operations of religion up till now. For example, we do not recognize something in the following text, which we always simply pass off as something about "morality," rather than a revelation and dislodgment of every sacrificial cult: "*So if you are offering your gift at the altar and there remember that your brother has something against you, leave your offering at the altar and go reconcile with your brother; then return and present your offering*" [Mt 5.23–24].

As long as the sacrificial cult guaranteed peace among brothers, it held sway; one could not speak as Christ does. But sacrifice has lost its power and it is Christ who finalizes that loss with the definitive revelation of a nonviolent god, in depriving humans of their last ritual crutches. We have to be reconciled without sacrifice or perish.

To see this is to understand the why and wherefore of the Kingdom of God. The Kingdom is perfect reciprocity, nothing more and nothing less. As long as men are raucously calling one another to account, there is no good reciprocity; the only good reciprocity is attained at the cost of totally renouncing violence, which is to say offering one's self as victim. In the world inaugurated by Christ, the world where revelation, however misunderstood, corrodes the structures of every society little by little, acting like a slow but inexorable plague, we are always approaching the moment when there will no longer be a choice between total destruction and this total renunciation of violence, the model offered by Christ.

This is quite obvious. And it is no less obvious that if men agree to turn the other cheek, if they accept to offer themselves as victims, there will be no victims. If, to the contrary, men refuse the message of peace, they will fall back into their accustomed ways of doing things. In yielding to the volatile spiral of violence, they are bound to return to the collective transfer on a unique victim. That is what happens to Christ and has everything to do with the revelation of violence but has no bearing directly with the kind of divinity attributed to him.

If we are dealing yet again with the violent sacred, the crucifixion would be effective at the social level. But Christ keeps telling us that it is not; quite to the contrary, the crucifixion entirely upsets social life, religious, and even familial life. Far from uttering threats about anything at all, Christ only spells out the consequences of this subversion. The gods of violence are demonetized by the announcement of a god of love; the machine has broken down, the expulsion no longer works. The murderers of Christ have acted in vain, or rather they have helped Christ to register the objective truth of violence into the gospel texts; and that truth, even if it is misrecognized or scorned, is going to slowly make its way, disintegrating everything like an insidious poison. That is precisely why Christ can say: "*I have not come to bring peace, but a sword. For I have come to oppose the son to his father, the daughter to her mother and the daughter-in-law to her mother-in-law; you will have foes in your own family*" [Mt 10.34–35].

To believe, like Ernest Renan, that the kingdom is "utopian" is excusable in his time, in a world swollen with pride and believing itself invulnerable, but to say as people do nowadays that "turning the other cheek" is "merely masochism" amounts to a refusal to see the kind of relations building up among us. Christ is the last messenger who came first to recall to the Jews first, then to the rest of the world, that reconciliation is the only way to pull through. The choice is simple: Either we all head out together toward the kingdom or we all head out together toward death.

The choice between the pronouncement of the kingdom on the one hand, on the other the passion and the apocalypse, is not problematic except for the exegetes who sacralize everything because they have as much confidence in their own society as in their own innocence. But people like Bultmann and other exegetes who want to be in the know have not yet realized this. They urge us to dismiss the apocalyptic theme as an old Jewish superstition that they say has nothing to do with how to think about matters. They always see "divine vengeance" in the apocalypse, something that the Old Testament had not yet jettisoned and that Western theology has hastened to reintroduce; but this does not figure importantly in the gospels. In Matthew 24, we are in no wise dealing with a god who would "avenge" the murder of his son, who would make men pay for a death that, with an extra measure of horror, he himself would have demanded. We are only dealing with intestine conflict and violent reciprocity, brother against brother and nation against nation.

Christ must die because he is the only one to follow the requirement of absolute nonviolence in a world that remains violent. In him, then, violence finds a victim who is no longer arbitrary but extremely significant because he is opposed to the regime of violence. On this point, the logic is the same as we find in *Antigone*, and here too Simone Weil has detected it. Antigone's refusal to comply with Creon's edict, by validating the least "difference" between the twins, the enemy brothers, must lead to her death. We could even say that Antigone also announces the kingdom when she declares her distrust in the gods of vengeance and asserts: "*I was born to share in love, not in hate.*" We can see in her, as in Christ, at once the greatest violence and no violence at all since she deprives men of the safety they seek in violence, of any sacrificial connivance.

But Antigone is evidently only a first draft, lacking a connection to the especially negative and still more potent efficacity of Christianity on the cultural and even planetary level. Who can fail to see the startling relevance of a desacralized apocalyptic theme that is linked to a science that in turn correlates with Judeo-Christian desacralization? To say that I am resuscitating ancestral terrors is frivolous. As for terror, one could do no better than the daily newspaper and the predictions of our scientists. Today, definitive violence, the truth of human history, is circulating all around us and over our heads like satellites, and it is capable of ending human history in a flash if we continue in this fashion. The specialists tell us without batting an eye that this violence alone protects us. We can no longer elude understanding how people could throw their own children into the furnace of the god Moloch, believing that in so doing they were protected against a worse violence.

In an essential way, our global society, all of humanity rounded up for the first time, finds itself in the same situation as the most fragile and impoverished primitive societies. We can destroy ourselves. By contrast, in another way our situation is very different: We are no longer endowed with instinctual brakes to intraspecific aggression, nor even the religious and collective ones. We are long past ritual gatherings around collective victims, which require *giving free rein* to violence in order to work properly, in order that it first reach a certain paroxysm. Science forbids this free play of violence by reason of the outlandish instruments it puts at our disposal. If we let loose only slightly, we will perish entirely. Even if snippets of sacralization cling to the gospel texts, my reading is too compelling, with respect both to the gospel texts and to present historical reality, to dismiss these structural correspondences as a matter of chance.

The Christian apocalyptic theme concerns human, not divine, terror, and its triumph is all the more probable because humanity has rid itself of the sacred bogey men that our humanists thought they had pulverized on their own and that they accuse Judeo-Christianity of proliferating. Well, we are well rid of them now. We know that we are entirely on our own, without any celestial punisher to trouble our petty concerns. So we have to look forward, not back; we have to face what humans are capable of. The decisive apocalyptic discourse tells us hardly anything else but the absolute responsibility of humans in history: You wanted to be left alone in your abode; *well, now it is in your hands*.

As soon as we substitute the nonsacrificial perspective from the traditional theological and anti-theological ones, we see the gospel themes spelled out logically: the crisis in Judaism, the kingdom, the passion, the double apocalypse, that of the Jews first and then of the gentiles, which historical Christianity has for a long time interpreted sacrificially. All this concerns the inevitable but gradual collapse of any sacrificial protection; all this is caused by the revelation of the god of the gospels.

And that is not all. If we look forward or backward, this interpretation of the gospel message as the destruction of the violent sacred is a source of insight. By its light, the Old Testament appears truly as an infinitely laborious *exodus* from sacrifice, culminating in the anti-sacrificial prophets, and within this tradition, the extraordinary *Servant Songs of Yahweh;* here we find for the first time the emergence into broad daylight of the mechanism of the unique victim. It is an emergence that takes place only there and nowhere else, in the same way that a scientific truth emerges at a given time in a certain text, and it matters little if no one is there to understand or confirm it. In Greek culture, at a time that corresponds to Second Isaiah, there are, with the pre-Socratics, with the tragedians, foreshadowing murmurs, but the revelation ultimately fails. *Truth comes from the Jews.*

That same revelation fails, of course, even among the Jews at the social level. It succeeds only on the level of the text; it is still there and we can always refer back to it. The only pre-scientific reading of the relations between the *Old* and *New Testaments* is to be found neither among our philosophers, Hegelian or other, nor among the erudite positivists of the last two centuries, but in New Testament *allegory*, patristic and even medieval, which is disdained these days. But this tradition alone has been able, in its best instances, to high-light the perfectly real concordances among the diverse in-stances where sacrifice is a problem, even though they could not always account for their own intuitions.

If we return to our starting point in the light of these ob-servations, we can no longer believe that it is we who read the gospels in the light of an ethnological and modern revelation that would be foremost. We have to reverse that order; it is always the great Judeo-Christian impetus that is driving the reading. All our ethnological knowledge makes sense in the light of ongoing revelation, of an immense historical undertaking that allows us to catch up little by little with texts that in fact are already explicit, but not for people such as we, *who have eyes not to see and ears not to hear.*

By a spectacular reversal, texts going back twenty and twenty-five centuries, first blindly venerated and these days rejected, are alone capable of fully revealing everything that is good and true in modern anti-Christian research, namely, the as yet still powerless determination to break with sacred violence. The biblical texts provide that research with what has been missing in order to furnish a radically sociological reading of all the historical forms of transcendence, and in the same stroke they position their own transcendence in a place that is inaccessible to any critique because it is from this place that all critique arises.

The gospels proclaim relentlessly this reversal of all interpretation. After telling the parable of the tenants of the vineyard who *unite to expel* the messengers of the owner, then murder his son in order become sole owners, Christ proposes to his hearers a problem of Old Testament exegesis: Jesus looked directly at them and asked, "*Then what is the meaning of that which is written: 'The stone the builders rejected has become the keystone?'*" [Mt 21.42].

These words come from Psalm 118 (117). Too many people supposed that Jesus's question calls for some "mystical" responses, not to be taken seriously on the level of the only knowledge that matters. Antireligious as well as modern religious thinkers are agreed as to that.

If all human religions and ultimately all human culture lead back to the parable of the murderous tenants, namely, the collective expulsion of victims, and if this founding principle is foundational only if it does not appear, it is clear that only the texts where this founding principle appears will not be founded in it and are truly revelatory. The sentence from Psalm 118 is therefore of prodigious epistemological value. It calls for an interpretation that Jesus ironically claims for himself, knowing full well that he alone can supply it by allowing himself to be rejected; by becoming himself the rejected stone, he shows that there has always been such a stone and that its founding role was hidden. Now this is revealed, such that it can no longer found anything, or rather that it founds something radically different. The proof that the gospels genuinely fulfill these words consists in the fact that the violent foundation of all religion makes its appearance in plain language in the passion of Christ and that it can no longer found anything.

Ultimately, the problem of exegesis posed by Christ can only be resolved if one sees in the words he quotes the exact prescription of the reversal that I am proposing. By undergoing violence to the bitter end, Christ reveals and uproots the structural matrix of all religion, even if, in the eyes of a less rigorous critique, the gospels are seen to favor only a new production of the matrix.

Ultimately, the text informs us of its own exegetical functioning, which breaks away from the rules of ordinary textuality, and it does so by this very informing, as its message eludes Christ's listeners. If this is the action of the text, the claims of Christianity to make of Christ the universal revealer are much more well founded than its defenders themselves imagine, by which I mean those who always blend elements of ordinary sacralization into Christian apologetics. As a result, they invariably regress to protocols of ordinary textuality; they once again erase the true origin that is nonetheless written in plain language in Scripture; they reject yet again, in a final and paradoxical expulsion, the stone that is Christ, and they continue not to see that that very same stone, as rejected, serves as their hidden keystone.

A Scientific Discourse

François Aubral: You know my questions.[2] Some problems still remain. I wonder if your idea of undifferentiation has not serious epistemological consequences. In effect, it allows you to develop an epistemology where we cannot distinguish anything, I mean an epistemology that constantly plays on the ambiguity between overlapping levels. I note the following: You speak of violence (in your own words) as a "universal model," of "founding" violence that you consider "essential" in the passage from the nonhuman to the human, "the founding event"; out of that you construct a theory that you call "unitary and properly totalizing," capable of "deconstructing all hermeneutics," a veritable "keystone." In spite of all that, you assert the "invisible" character of violence that nonetheless allows you to set up a scientific theory in the full sense of the word. Now, I am worried. I wonder if the least exception (such as Michel Panoff might find in ethnology) might be capable of ruining the epistemological coherence of your system: What are the primary data for your violent epistemology, which seems to me to sacrifice all science? Can we speak on the same level of a literary text, of a myth, of an ethnological fact, and of a theory? Are you not searching in violence for a kind of universal feature that had not been found in other bygone systems? Finally, is there not, underlying your discourse, an essentialist ideology that calls for a fixed point, an absolute, a kind of God?

René Girard: There is an absolutely fundamental misunderstanding here: Everything you have said, everything that you have quoted about violence, consists in a reading of the sacred that we find in myth and in culture. I am saying that violence is no longer foundational; it has always been so, but obviously I am not founding anything on it.

François Aubral: We have to look at the status of that notion . . .

René Girard: The status of that notion is, precisely, the sacred. I am tempted to say we remain pervaded by the sacred, but I do not want to misconstrue your question.

François Aubral: Yes, but what then is the status of a scientific discourse? Where does it comes from? What is it? When there is a problem in ethnology, your answer is about literature; when there is a problem in literature, you answer with pre-Socratics, etc. I do not maintain that philosophical texts and literary texts should be compartmentalized, but the way you do not differentiate between them raises a serious question of interpretation.

René Girard: From the perspective with which I began (I acknowledge the difficulty of having to take on too many huge questions so briskly), I will say this about my hypothesis on the origin of culture: We have to see if it organizes the data in a way that is more coherent than others. If your answer is "no," I acknowledge that what I am arguing is absolutely without merit. If your answer is "yes" . . .

François Aubral: I am with you on that! We have to be integrally with you, not halfway.

René Girard: There is perhaps a middle ground, but I find it impossible to conceive of one.

Jean-Marie Domenach: It's like lynching.

François Aubral: Pretty soon you're going to use Judeo-Christianity to show how, within the myths it produces, it sets itself apart and has universalizing value. The most elementary epistemology does not allow for such reductiveness. That is enormous.

René Girard: In fact, it is enormous. The immense task of anthropology has been entirely directed, we must remember, against the claims of Judeo-Christianity, and, in a certain sense, with good reason since it was always targeting sacrificial—therefore fallacious—interpretations of its texts. What extraordinary irony there is if Judeo-Christianity suddenly leads, at the moment of accomplishing its objective, to a confirmation of these same claims, and in a manner as resounding as it is unexpected.

Modern thought would then do well to think about those numerous desert excavators in Second Isaiah, about all those slaves, supplied of course these days with magnificent bulldozers, who don't know why the mountains are being leveled and the valleys filled with such unusual frenzy. They have barely heard about this great king who is going to pass in triumph on the road they are preparing.

Among us, we are often told, scandal alone has value; we have to think scandalously. Finally we have something other than the old scandals reheated many times over, à la de Sade and Nietzsche, the old romantic follies boringly recycled. Here is something to send shudders through a modernity known to be avid for sensations. Here is a brand new, nice big scandal for the end of the twentieth century. It is a good bet that it will have no success, that for as long as possible people will find a way to make it disappear.

Everything in our culture suggests that I am out of my mind. But let's stop a moment to consider the present state of this culture. It has invented ethnology, the science of myths, psychoanalysis. This same culture finds itself periodically jolted by "apocalyptic" crises. The last one has been going on for more than a quarter century; it is surely the most severe, the most agonizing, since the basics of the most "hard" sciences are strangely mixed up with some basics of traditional religion and the most grotesque superstitions.

Imagine intelligent observers from another planet of our little games. They would see veritable armies devoted to the study of social phenomena, to the interpretation of the least individual and collective reactions. They would take note of the prodigious importance that our intellectuals have attached for a century to old Greek stories of a man named Oedipus and one named Dionysus. They would measure the gigantic amount of work devoted to these characters, the quasi-religious respect that since the sixteenth century has surrounded the Greeks first of all, then primitive cultures in general. They would compare all that to the ongoing loss of interest paid to Judeo-Christianity, that is, to the texts that configurate—perhaps fancifully and deceptively, that's quite possible—a cogent and rigorous theory of the destruction of our entire world, one that is perfectly explicit and so necessarily significant for the delirium besieging us. And these same texts arise from no other religion than our own; for better or for worse, these texts have, up till now and perhaps going forward, dominated a movement that is taking us to the unknown. You might think that a society so keen on self-observation and self-understanding might detach a battalion from this great army, camped in the shade of Greek temples and Bororo villages, with a mission to find out if, as to Judeo-Christianity, everything has been said and done as we have imagined it.

Nothing doing, quite the contrary. If our thinking is no longer founded on the physical expulsion of violence, and of the truth of violence, we are experiencing a gigantic intellectual expulsion of Judeo-Christianity in its entirety, that is to say, among other things, the expulsion of all truly serious problematics of religion and culture; the expulsion is all the more systemic even as the growing risks of understanding increase, that is to say, even as our violence is fully revealed in history and technology.

This intellectual violence has not awaited the explicit repudiation of Judeo-Christianity to take wing, and we can see in it a recapitulation, paradoxically, of all human religion. What is expelled from our religion is unlike all the other; this time the truth about humanity is not expelled indirectly but quite directly. What is expelled is the burden of a truth so strong, its return is such a threat to us that we think we can manage very well by a more thorough expulsion of all religious problematics. Primitive religion can only perpetuate itself by expelling all religion. It is the expulsion of the Johannine Logos itself, not that of Heraclitus with which we have always confused it, but the Johannine Logos that is absolutely distinct from it.

This confusion is already the expulsion of the Johannine Logos. At a time when philosophy aspired to be Christian, it proclaimed the essential identity of the two Logos, the Greek one appearing as the prophetic "prefiguration" of Judeo-Christianity. Modern erudition has inverted the relationship but conserved it. The Logos of Heraclitus has taken first place and the Johannine Logos figures only as a pale imitation. Christianity henceforth makes its appearance as the blue jay sporting the feathers of the Greek peacock.

Heidegger finds that we still grant too much to the Johannine Logos (*Introduction to Metaphysics*). Even if one does not agree with his definition of the latter, the one he gives for the Logos of Heraclitus should ultimately lead to the truth. The Logos of Heraclitus, he says, holds opposites together, and not without violence. That much is quite explicit. The Logos of Heraclitus is the Logos of expulsion, the Logos of the polis closed around itself and subsequently that of modern nations, entrenched in one place only, in one language only. But even a child can discern that this Logos is not that of John, of which it is written: "*The light shines in the darkness and the darkness is dispelled. . . . He came among his own and his own did not receive him.* [Jn 1, 5, 11]."

The Logos of Heraclitus established itself as such by erasing somehow the traces of expulsion, while the Johannine Logos will succeed in finally revealing that same expulsion, because, in the final analysis, it is always this Logos that undergoes expulsion. It is always this Logos that suffers misrecognition, parasitically disfigured by the other Logos, first in order to protect men from tearing one another apart and then to slowly reveal itself to them by a process that is indirect. It is indirect in that it only attracts humans towards good reciprocity by destroying little by little all the myths of violence, by gradually depriving the other Logos of all sacrificial prospects, of everything that allows us to disguise it; and, by a counterstroke, it abolishes any limit to our own violence.

François Aubral: What I do not understand—but this would be a question for an ethnologist—is how we can determine that a certain body of texts, those of Judeo-Christianity, should be analyzed in a different way than others and should be granted a privileged status that endows them with a specific and universal value.

René Girard: You tell me that we have to follow science to decrypt cultural texts. But your science is never anything but yet another series of texts. So I turn your question back to you: Why privilege all these other texts rather than mine. Is it because they present themselves as *scientific*, because everyone around you "believes in psychoanalysis," or in structuralism, as they used to believe in religion? I do not want to believe that. You need better reasons than those. Everywhere there is science, there are hypotheses whose value is measured by the results they produce. Personally,

I think that the hypotheses you judge respectable have not fulfilled their promises, so I think we must no longer respect them. If the gospels appear to me to be more fruitful than the texts of Freud in terms of ethnological data, I will follow the gospels even if they contradict Freud. The most knowledgeable text is not necessarily the one we take as such. You want to impose a distinction between a scientific text and a nonscientific text that strikes me as invidious and contrary to a true scientific spirit.

You tell me that a singular exception would oblige me to abandon my theory. You are right, it is on that ground that we must place ourselves. We must provide concrete facts and see whether or not the hypothesis passes this test. But it is altogether something else to say: That works too well to be true. If I were collecting data around a general idea, in the manner of philosophers, I would understand that one could say that; but my work is focused on a definite sociological mechanism in a manner that is quite precise. Under these conditions it strikes me as antiscientific to reject a thesis *because it works*. It must be rejected if, on the contrary, it can be shown that it does not work.

Notes

1. Trans. note: Empedocles proposed elemental forces he called Love and Strife, which would mix and separate the elements, respectively.

2. François Aubral is alluding to his critique of *Violence and the Sacred* published in *Les Cahiers du chemin*, no. 17.

Appendix: Table of Passages

The following table highlights the passages from the "Discussion with René Girard" (1973) that Girard reused, most frequently without the slightest amendments, for *Things Hidden Since the Foundation of the World* (1978). Given the differences between Andrew J. McKenna's outstanding translation ("Discussion") and that of Stephen Bann and Michael Metteer (*Things Hidden*), the listed passages may not strike as identical to English readers. This table may be taken as a possible starting point for a comparative reading of the "Discussion" and *Things Hidden*. It may further help with comparing the translations into English. For the first two columns of the table, readers are invited to review the passage starting with the first part of the quote in the cell and ending with what follows the ellipsis dots.

This appendix was authored by Andreas Wilmes.

"Discussion with René Girard," this volume	Things Hidden Since the Foundation of the World (New York: Bloomsbury, 2016)	Pages from the French Editions
"The gospels situate themselves explicitly at the paroxysm of a crisis . . . the vertiginous effect of violence." (50)	"The gospels show themselves to be placed at the paroxysm of the crisis . . . not succumbing to the escalating violence." (191–192)	"Discussion avec René Girard," *Esprit* 11 (November 1973), 551. *Des choses cachées depuis la fondation du monde* (Paris: LGF, 1983), 276.
"To believe, like Ernst Renan . . . among us." (57)	Very slightly amended: "A world that was swollen with pride and thought itself invulnerable could still believe with Renan, that the Kingdom is 'Utopian.' But people who say nowadays that the gospel principle of non-reprisal is 'only masochism' fail to reflect the constraints that weigh heavily upon us [que fait déjà peser sur nous et que fera de plus en plus peser] as a result of our excessive power of destruction." (248)	"Discussion," 554. *Des choses cachées*, 350

"Discussion with René Girard," this volume	Things Hidden Since the Foundation of the World (New York: Bloomsbury, 2016)	Pages from the French Editions
"The Christian apocalyptic theme concerns human, not divine, terror . . . *well, now it is in your hands*." (60–61)	"The theme of the Christian Apocalypse involves human terror . . . *well then, it is given up to you*." (187)	"Discussion," 556. *Des choses cachées*, 270.
"If we return to our starting point . . . '*who have eyes not to see and ears not to hear*.'" (62–63)	"We can no longer believe that . . . *who have eyes and see not, ears and hear not*." (170)	"Discussion," 557. *Des choses cachées*, 248.
"By a spectacular reversal, . . . something radically different." (63–65)	"By an astonishing reversal . . . something that is radically different." (170–171)	"Discussion," 557–558. *Des choses cachées*, 248–249.
"Ultimately, the problem of exegesis . . . serves as their hidden keystone." (65–66)	"The problem of exegesis . . . as a concealed cornerstone." (171–172)	"Discussion," 558. *Des choses cachées*, 249–250.
"The immense task of anthropology . . . on the road they are preparing (69–70)	"It is extremely ironic . . . the road they are preparing for him." (267)	"Discussion," 560. *Des choses cachées*, 375.

"Discussion with René Girard," this volume	Things Hidden Since the Foundation of the World (New York: Bloomsbury, 2016)	Pages from the French Editions
"Among us, we are often told, scandal alone . . . find a way to make it disappear." (70)	"We are told that scandal . . . conjure it away for as long as they possibly can." (267)	"Discussion," 560. *Des choses cachées*, 375.
"Everything in our culture suggests . . . our violence is fully revealed in history and technology." (70–72)	"All the voices of our culture conspire . . . the self-revelation of violence, in history and technology." (250–251)	"Discussion," 561. *Des choses cachées*, 352–353.

Index